Creating Lampwork
Beads for Jewelry

By Karen J. Leonardo

©2007 by Karen J. Leonardo

Published by

krause publications

An Imprint of F+W Publications

700 East State Street • Iola, WI 54990-0001
715-445-2214 • 888-457-2873
www.krausebooks.com

Our toll-free number to place an order or obtain a free catalog is (800) 258-0929.

The following trademarked terms and companies appear in this publication:

Beadalon®, Czech beads, E 6000®, Effetre Glass, Hot Head Torch, Moretti, Sculpey® Bake and Bend, Swarovski®

Library of Congress Catalog Number: 2007924542

ISBN-13: 978-0-89689-549-2
ISBN-10: 0-89689-549-1

Designed by Rachael Knier
Edited by Erica Swanson

Printed in China

Every effort has been made to ensure that instructions are accurate. However, due to differing equipment and technique, the publisher and author are not responsible for any injuries or damages resulting from information found in this book. It is up to the reader to follow manufacturer's instructions and review the safety checklist on pg. 17.

ACKNOWLEDGMENTS

I would like to dedicate this book to the memory of my grandmother, Mary Krisay. She was the rock of our family when my mother passed away when I was a young girl. Her love and support allowed me to pursue my dreams and see them come true!

I would like to thank God because he makes ALL things possible!

I also want to thank my family: my husband Bob, and my children, Brock, Erica and Braden, for their continual support of my endeavors. I cannot forget my wonderful mother-in-law, Barb, for picking up where I leave off. Thanks to all the lampworkers for their beautiful contributions: Bob Leonardo, Leslie Kaplan, Kristan Child, Cathy Lybarger, Christine Schneider, Cindy Palmer, JC Herrell, Sue Booth, Lezlie Belanger and Amy Cornett. Thanks to all of the designers who made gorgeous jewelry pieces from the beads: Sue Hart, Cary Martin, Robin Bond, Joyce Facchiano, Nora Howe and Cindy Vela. A special thanks to Amy Cornett and Joyce Facchiano for all of the extras. Sue Hart has been my rock, and I thank her for not only contributing and taking many pictures, but also for being such a wonderful friend and taking on all the challenges I throw her way. Thanks to Brian Helgerson from Sundance Art Glass, who took all the pictures in the first two chapters and really pulled through when life was difficult.

A very special thanks to a very good friend, Susan Ray, who made this book possible; without her it would not have been written. Susan, you have been an awesome mentor. Thanks go out to Lisa Liddy who put everything in order for me with such patience and encouragement. I'm so glad that we met. It has been an enriching experience, and I appreciate all you have done to get this book together for me. Thanks to Candy Wiza, the acquisitions editor, for the extra time you spent walking me through the proposal. Thanks to my editor, Erica Swanson, for leading the way and coaching me through the book process. Thanks to designer Rachael Knier and photographer Kris Kandler, who helped make this book a reality. Thanks again to everyone for making my dreams come true!

TABLE OF CONTENTS

FOREWORD

Glass beads are magical. They are tiny worlds where viewers can lose themselves in the intricacy and depth of a piece of wearable art. Making glass beads is doubly magical. As bead makers, we get to watch them grow and change in the torch as they are created. We're alchemists, turning basic materials into something of great value.

When Karen first approached me to write the foreword to her book, her eyes shone with so much energy and excitement, I couldn't wait to see the project that had her all fired up. The wait was worth it! This beautiful book promises to be a staple for every lampworker and designer's collection.

The bead tutorials are well-written and easy to follow, and they increase in difficulty and complexity, so that one is constantly challenged and inspired. Each lesson is enhanced by Karen's unique skill and knowledge of metals and reactive glass. Besides the beautifully presented tutorials for the torch, "Creating Lampwork Beads for Jewelry" solves the common dilemma of many a lampworker, by showing us what to do with these works of art after they've been completed. It moves beyond the bead and into the realm of the jewelry artist. Here again, Karen has outdone herself by inviting exciting and creative artists to share in her vision. The designs range from simple and elegant, to complex and edgy. There is something here to inspire everyone.

Karen has invited the reader to travel with ease through every step on the way to creating beautiful lampwork beads and jewelry. Enjoy the ride!

—Jennifer Geldard

Jennifer Geldard is an internationally-known lampwork artist and instructor whose beads are collected around the world. She has been making glass beads and sculpture since 1994.

Jennifer's work can be seen on her Web site, http://www.glassgirl.com.

INTRODUCTION

Maybe you are a jewelry designer who has always wanted to learn how to make your own lampwork beads — or maybe you are new to lampworking and would like to learn the secrets of the art from some of the skilled lampworkers out there today. This book will take you through each step.

I will teach you how to set up your own basic lampwork beadmaking studio for soft glass and borosilicate glass, and I will also walk you through making your first lampwork bead. Then, it's time to play with intermediate and advanced techniques. You will use various frits and latticino, and make custom colors and special shapes. You can create an ancient metallic disc, an implosion bead, and a mask bead with handmade eyeball murrini and cane. Once you practice making these beads, you can find your own style and make them unique by adding other techniques.

Perhaps you have been lampworking for years but would like to learn how to make jewelry out of your beads. Once you have created the beads, you will want to use them in new, exciting jewelry designs. You will learn how to set up a jewelry studio and use the tools you will need to get started. Build your basic toolbox, and make a special jewelry space just for you. Designers will share some of their basic jewelry-making tips and secrets on wire forming.

There is a resource page in the back of the book that tells you where you can buy supplies and equipment, ask for extra instruction through various help sites, or buy the beads or jewelry that you see. There is something in this book for everyone! So, what are you waiting for? It's time to jump right in and get started!

—Karen

Chapter 1
Setting Up Your Studio

The first thing you need to do is get organized. This means setting up a space where you can work comfortably and safely. When you choose the area that you will use as a lampwork studio, think about the space where you will be creating your beads: Is it large enough? Does the room have ventilation? Is the lighting adequate? Is the chair the right size, and does it fit the table well? Are there any potential safety hazards?

Once you have chosen a space, you can begin organizing the supplies you will need. Since you will be working with fire, work on a non-flammable surface, like a table covered with stainless steel sheeting. You will need a small space the size of a card table (it is best not to make beads on your nice dining room table, even with the protective sheeting). Be sure the table is sturdy and that there are no flammables in your space.

CHOOSING A KIT

There are two types of kits available. If you have never tried beadmaking before, you might want to choose the inexpensive beginner kit. A basic beginner kit has everything you need to make your first beads out of soft glass, except for the MAPP gas bottle (discussed later) and glass. There are some companies that include the glass with the basic kit and offer add-ons like strikers, rod nippers, parallel mashers, mini mashers and looped hemostats.

MAPP Gas Set-up

The basic kit includes:

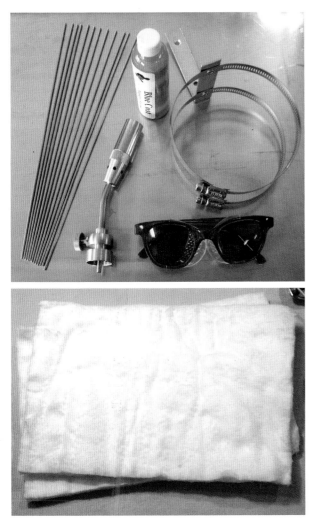

- A torch (I like the Hot Head torch)
- A bracket holder or work surface
- Didymium safety glasses
- Mandrels
- Bead release
- Ceramic fiber blanket
- Sample pack of soft glass

I would also suggest purchasing looped hemostats for holding small pieces of glass and a graphite marvering paddle for shaping glass. To use your torch, simply screw it on a MAPP gas cylinder, following manufacturer's instructions.

Attach the MAPP gas tank and holder to the table with a C-clamp.

OXYGEN AND PROPANE SET-UP

An intermediate kit for soft glass or beginner kit for hard glass (borosilicate) includes everything in the basic kit except the Hot Head Torch, plus these additional items:

- Oxygen and propane burner torch (such as a Minor Bench Burner)
- Oxygen regulator and hose (green)
- Propane regulator and hose (red)
- Flashback arrestors

If you want to try borosilicate glass (boro), you will need to purchase some boro as well. It comes in sample packs with various colors. When working boro, you will also need special glasses called boroscope lenses to protect your eyes from the bright glare of the melting glass.

You will need a C-clamp to clamp your torch to the table, as well as special cording, such as bungee cord, rope or chain to tie your tanks to the table or wall.

The oxygen and propane set-up uses oxygen as your accelerant and propane as your fuel.

Call your local welding supplier or gas supplier to purchase or rent an oxygen tank. You can use your barbeque grill propane tank if you do not want to purchase another propane tank for beadmaking. If you are nervous about setting up your torch and gases, have your gas supplier set up your tanks, hoses and regulators. He can also show you how to turn your tanks on and off, and tell you about important safety precautions and local regulations.

Setting up your Oxygen/Propane System with the Minor Burner:

1. Follow manufacturer's instructions to set up your torch. Attach the red hose to the top connection on your torch (the red knob), and tighten the hose-fitting sleeve clamp. Red hose = propane.

2. Attach the green hose to the bottom connection on the torch, and tighten the hose-fitting sleeve clamp. Silver knob = oxygen.

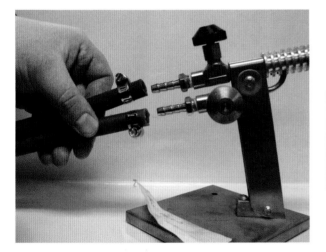

3. Attach the flashback arrestors to the proper regulators and the other end of the hoses. The flashback arrestors are gold cylinders. The propane arrestor has a red line and the oxygen arrestor has a green line.

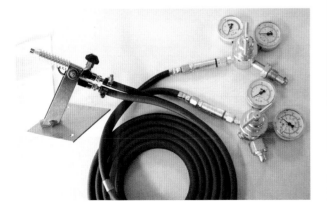

4. Attach the propane regulator to the propane tank. The threads are reverse threads, so you can't mix them up. Be sure to tighten the clamps well so that propane can't escape, but don't tighten so well that you will never be able to remove them. Open the propane tank valve. If you hear a hissing sound, smell propane after 10 minutes or more, or see the pressure drop, the clamps are not tight enough.

5. Attach the oxygen regulator to the oxygen tank, and tighten well. Open the valve to allow oxygen through. Check for a pressure drop or hissing sounds to be sure that there is no leak.

After making sure that your connections fit properly, it is time to light the torch.

Igniting the Hot Head Torch

To light the MAPP gas Hot Head torch, hold the striker or match 3" to 4" from the head of the torch, turn the knob to the left slightly to open the valve, and ignite. If you are having difficulty lighting the torch, turn the MAPP gas up a bit more. If you are using a striker, some of the gas should catch in the cup and ignite.

There will be a "poof" as the gas lights. Turn the knob to the right to shut it off.

Setting Your Torch Valves

Now that you have attached your hoses and regulators, you will need to set your regulators and turn on your torch. First, open both tank valves. You will see the pressure jump up on the regulators. This shows you how much propane and oxygen you have in the tanks. Turn the T-bar on the regulator to the right to tighten and allow the pressure to build up. Set to your desired pressure. Do the same for the propane.

PRESSURE CHART

Soft glass	Boro
Oxygen 10 to 20 psi	Oxygen 15 to 25 psi
Propane 2 to 5 psi	Propane 5 to 10 psi

Now that your valves are set, you are ready to light the torch.

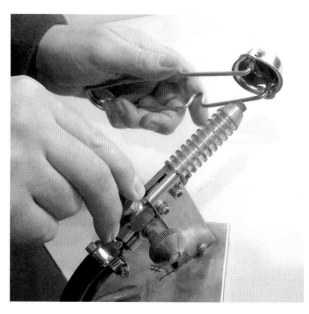

TIP:

Before igniting your Hot Head torch or Minor Bench Burner, practice making sparks with your striker. It is not as easy as you might think!

Also, be sure that the tank valves are open and the pressure is set correctly for your type of glass.

Have your flint striker ready and turn the red knob (propane) to the left (counter-clockwise) just enough to light the torch. If you use too much gas, you will have a huge flame. If you don't use enough gas, it won't light. When you have a small flame (about 4"), turn on the oxygen slowly by turning the silver knob toward you and increasing the amount of oxygen until you see a small white cone in the middle of the flame. It should be about ¼", and the whole flame should be 6"–8" long. You may need to adjust your propane or oxygen if the flame seems too strong or the inner cone is too small or large. If you are new to the surface-mixed fuel system, you may want to work on the lower end of the scale and increase your propane and oxygen a bit after you start feeling comfortable working with the flame.

Now that you have successfully turned your torch on and know about the various flames, turn it off properly and depressurize the valves. First, turn off the oxygen valve by turning the silver knob away from you. When you do this, the flame will be bushy; you can turn the red propane knob to the right (clockwise) to shut it off and extinguish the flame. Loosen the T-bar on your propane and oxygen by turning it to the left. You will lose pressure until the gauge reads 0. Bleed the lines (empty the remaining gas and oxygen in the lines) by turning the torch valves to release the extra gases. Be sure to close your torch valves when you are done, or they will lose pressure and hiss when you pressurize the tanks again. Close the propane and oxygen tank valves.

A great way to remember how to turn your torch on and off is the POOP rule, which I first learned from Cindy Jenkins, and she gives credit to Bandhu Scott Dunham. Follow this rule when turning your torch on and off:

Propane turn on first.
Oxygen turn on last.
Oxygen shut off first.
Propane shut off last.

Congratulations! You have successfully learned how to use your torch. Now let's talk about another important piece of equipment for beadmaking: the kiln.

The left flame shows an oxidation flame, the middle flame is the working flame or neutral flame, and the flame on the right shows a reduction flame. You will most likely work your bead at the tip of the inner cone in the middle flame.

CHOOSING A KILN

A kiln is an insulated container that controls a high-heat environment. It allows you to maintain a consistent temperature and then slow cool your bead so it does not crack from thermal shock. Holding your bead at a temperature for a given amount of time is called annealing. The temperature and time for annealing depends on the size of bead. Some beginner beadmakers put their beads in ceramic fiber blankets to slow cool them and anneal them properly in a kiln later; others put the mandrel and hot bead directly into the kiln right away. Placing beads directly into the kiln is recommended.

There are many kilns on the market in all price ranges and for all skill levels. Before you purchase a kiln, ask yourself these questions:

- Am I only interested in annealing beads, or do I want to learn how to fuse glass or make larger sculptures in the future?
- Do I want to be able to leave the kiln and not worry if I turned it off or not?
- Do I want to invest in a digital controller?
- Do I want a top loader, side loader or portable kiln?
- Do I want to plug it into a household 120 volt socket?

Decide which features are important to you, and research to find the kiln that meets your needs.

As you consider which kiln to buy, consider these amenities:

- The inner dimensions of the kiln
- How it opens; does it have a larger door and bead door?
- Whether the kiln has a pyrometer, infinite controller or digital controller
- Where the elements of the kiln are placed: top, sides or both
- What you will set your beads on: a built-in bead rack or kiln posts
- The maximum temperature the kiln can reach
- Whether the kiln is table-top or portable
- Whether the kiln uses electricity or gas (gas is less popular)
- Whether the kiln is for professional or hobby use
- Price; usually, smaller kilns are less expensive

TIP:

Purchase a kiln designed for glass, because ceramic kilns do not have the same safety features. You could stick your mandrels in a kiln where the elements are exposed and be electrocuted.

Kiln with internal bead rack.

Kiln Possibilities

Top-loader with bead door and digital controller.

Bead annealing kiln with infinite switch.

Beads in a side-loader with digital controller.

Chapter 2
Making Your First Bead

Before you begin creating your first bead, you need to know how to use the glass correctly. The Coefficient of Expansion (COE) tells you how the glass expands and contracts when heated and cooled. Each type of glass is given a number, and you should stay in that range when mixing glass so that the glass is compatible. Soft glass, such as Effetre and Reichenbach, has a higher COE than hard glass, like Pyrex and colored boro. Soft glass is easier to melt and manipulate in the flame than the hard glass. If you mix two incompatible glasses together, the bead will shatter or crack. For example, the COE of Effetre glass ranges from 104 to 108, and the COE of boro is about 32. You would not want to mix the glass together; although they will melt together, they will chip, shatter and crack when cool. Since most beads are small, you would be able to mix some Reichenbach glass COE 96 with the 104 Effetre. Experiment to see what works for you.

The color range is different for each type, although some companies are coming out with the unique, changing colors of boro in the soft glass COE range.

Generally, soft glass is less expensive than hard glass, unless you choose unique, reactive colors. When you are learning to make your first beads, it is best to start with the soft glass since it is much easier to melt and manipulate, it takes less time to make a bead and the flame is not as intense. Boro also requires extra fuel and oxygen to melt the glass.

PREPARING THE MANDRELS

You received bead release and mandrels in your kit. The bead release allows you to remove your beads from the mandrel when the bead is completed and has cooled. Each type of bead release is different, and beadmakers use different types. You will want to discover what works best for you. Preparing your mandrels is the easy part: just shake the bottle, dip the mandrel and set it in a container with sand to dry.

Make sure that you have enough release on the mandrel to remove the bead once it is cooled. Some bead release is flame-ready and can be used immediately; some needs time to dry completely, or it will crack off or bubble under the glass when heated in the flame. Be sure to read the manufacturer's directions first. Dip plenty of mandrels so that you have as many as you need for your session.

PREPARING YOUR WORKING SPACE

You are almost ready to make your beads, so prepare your work area. Set the tools you will use on the table on the side of your dominant hand. Lay them close to you so that you aren't reaching over the flame to grab them. Place your mandrels somewhere close for easy access, and put your glass next to your tools. Be sure that you have proper eye protection ready. If you are using any extra embellishments, prepare them before you begin making your beads. Have your frits, foils and enamels ready to go. Position your fiber blanket, or turn on your kiln and bring it to temperature. Check your tanks and gauges to be sure they are working properly.

Christine Schneider's professional lampwork studio.

Go through this list of safety precautions before beginning:

- Have your fire extinguisher ready.
- Keep flammables away from your working area.
- Remember that the torch is hot and will remain that way for a few minutes after you turn it off.
- As you work, be aware of your hot glass rod ends!
- Do not lean and look away from the flame when your hand is near, or your hand could end up in the flame.
- Keep burn cream handy.
- Do not leave your torch unattended.
- Be sure to pre-heat glass rods before placing them in the flame or they will shatter!

- Wear proper eye protection for whichever glass and torch you are using.
- Do not walk around in your studio barefoot.
- Be sure your area is well ventilated.
- Keep your area free from powders, enamels, pieces of fiber blanket or dust-carrying materials. They are a respiratory hazard. Use a certified respirator when needed.
- Add a carbon monoxide detector to the room.

Now it's time to start making your first bead!

Christine Schneider's professional lampwork studio.

MAKING THE BEAD

Supplies:

- ♦ Your torch
- ♦ A bracket holder or work surface
- ♦ Didymium safety glasses
- ♦ Mandrels
- ♦ Bead release
- ♦ Soft glass in color of your choice
- ♦ Ceramic fiber blanket

1. Turn on your torch, and use your dominant hand to preheat the tip of the glass rod in the edges of the flame. Do not place it directly in the flame or it will shatter. Next, heat the rod directly in the flame about ½", rotating it around to heat all sides. It should be a nice orange glow, with some movement but not fluid. You want the glass to be hot enough to stick to the mandrel, but not so drippy that you do not have control of it.

2. As you are heating the glass, add the mandrel to the flame and heat the area where you want to make your bead. You will see the dark color of the bead release turn a lighter color and glow a bit. Touch the hot tip of the glass to the mandrel.

3. Wrap the hot glass on the mandrel and, turning it away from you continually, rotate the mandrel. Pull away when you don't have any more hot glass to wrap.

4. Reheat the glass, and add more. You should always be rotating your mandrel so that gravity does not take over and cause hot glass to land on the table or in your lap. If the glass does not stick to the mandrel, either the mandrel or the tip of the glass is not hot enough yet. If you pulled the bead release from the mandrel, it could mean you were trying to wrap cold glass. If you have cold glass that won't come away from the mandrel, do not pull, but heat the cold glass near the bead until it melts off.

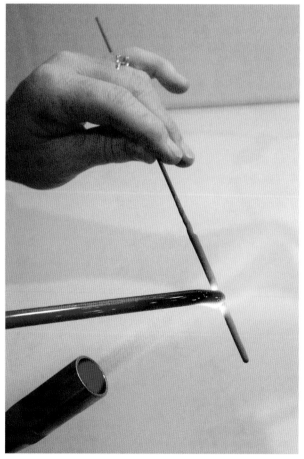

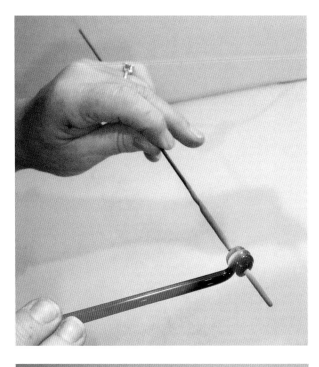

5. Rotate and heat the bead, and let gravity move the hot glass on the mandrel to shape your bead. Keep your mandrel horizontal unless you need to move a little bit of the glass to the right or left. Tilt the mandrel a bit, and heat the glass on the end where you want more shape — but continue to move the bead back and forth in the flame to keep the whole bead warm.

6. When you are satisfied with the shape of your bead, take it into the upper parts of the flame to flame anneal. Flame annealing allows you to heat your bead to a consistent temperature overall. Roll in the flame for a few seconds, or until it has been heated evenly, and then take it out of the flame. Wait a few seconds until the glow is gone, and put the bead into a fiber blanket or kiln. If your bead is too warm when you put it in the fiber blanket, it will come out dimpled and covered with fiber. If it is too cool, it will crack.

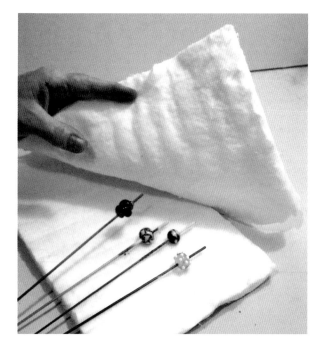

7. Allow your bead to slow cool in the fiber blanket for about an hour. If you want to sell your beads, you should anneal them properly in a kiln to reduce the stress within the glass. Even if beads don't show any cracks right now, they may crack later if not annealed in a kiln.

8. You may also put the beads directly into a kiln, which is the preferred method of annealing. As your beads become larger and more advanced, you will definitely want to purchase a kiln. If your beads are less than 2" thick, the kiln temperature for annealing Effetre glass is around 860 degrees Fahrenheit and 1040 degrees for boro. Some lampworkers use higher temperatures, but I have found these temperatures successful. If the kiln is hotter, the beads may stick together.

9. When finished annealing, carefully remove the beads from the kiln, slide them off the mandrel, and clean them. Hold the mandrel near the bead with a pair of pliers , running it in water and twisting as you pull. Be careful not to bend the mandrel when pulling and twisting the bead off. Some bead release is stubborn, so if you are not able to get the bead off, let it soak in warm water for 15 minutes. You will learn how to work the mandrel release in the flame to make it easier to remove your beads later — otherwise you will end up with beautiful plant sticks.

10. When you have removed the bead from the mandrel, clean the inside of the bead by running it under warm water and moving your mandrel in and out of the hole to remove some of the release. You can also purchase bead cleaners and reamers (thick wire the size of your bead hole with grooves or grit to remove bead release), or a motorized drill with the appropriate bits to clean the inside of your beads. Be careful when using a motorized bit, because if it is going too fast, it can chip the holes of your beads or even break off a whole chunk of your bead.

You have just completed your first bead! Congratulations! You will get better at the beadmaking process when you understand how to manipulate the flame and work the glass, and this can only be achieved with lots of practice. There are some simple beads with just a bit of decoration, and there are others that will require more skilled application, such as making twisted cane, adding metallic frits, and placing bubbles. Your friends will ask, "How did you do that?"

Let's get started!

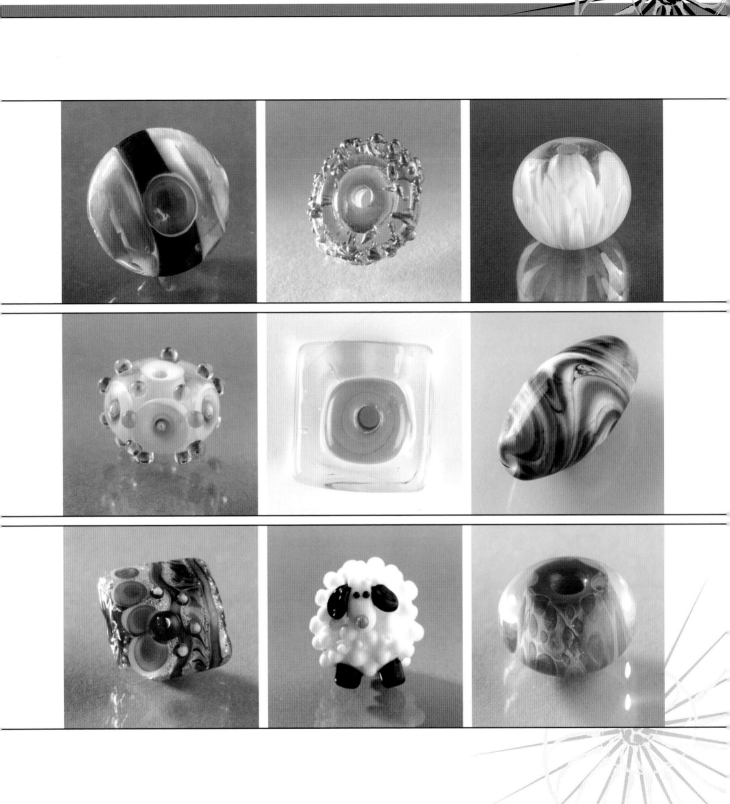

Chapter 3
Beads

• Lampwork Artist: Karen Leonardo • Style of Bead: Small Round with Twistie •
• Finished Size: 7 mm x 11 mm • Level of Expertise: Beginner •

Beach Twist

Beach twist beads are easy to make, and the colorful twistie bring a bright splash of color to a plain bead. A twistie is two rods of glass heated and twisted together as you pull them. Have fun in the sun with brilliant orange, yellow and green, or choose any colors you like. Put on your sandals and grab your sunglasses — it's time for a beach party!

SUPPLIES:

Effetre Orange #422
Effetre Bright Acid Yellow #416
Effetre Pea Green #212

TOOLBOX:

Tweezers

INSTRUCTIONS:

1. Tie the Orange and Yellow rods with a rubber band to hold them together. Melt the end of the two rods, and pinch the ends together with the tweezers.

Tie the rods together.

2. Melt the end. Bring the end out of the flame, but keep it close enough to slowly twist and pull. If the glass gets too hard to pull, flash it in the flame a bit. When cool, set aside.

Heat, pull and twist to make the twistie.

3. Make a small disc from the Pea Green glass. Melt down to give you even ends on the round bead.

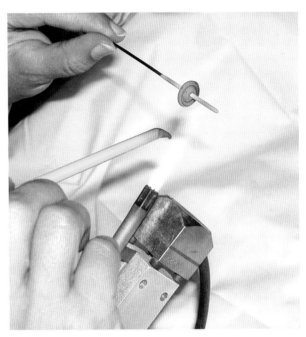

Wrap a disc.

4. Melt down to a round bead.

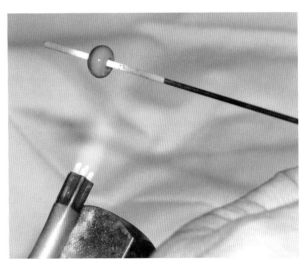

Melt down to a small round bead.

5. Heat and wrap the twistie. Melt in, and then flame anneal.

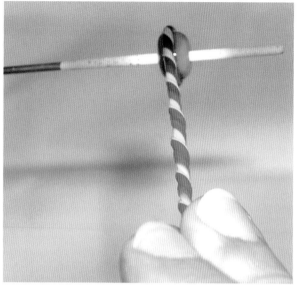

Wrap the twistie.

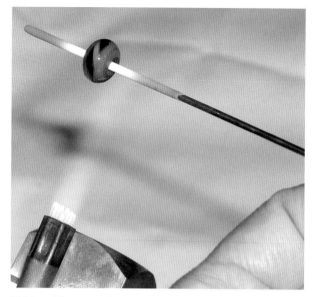

Melt in and flame anneal.

HOT GLASS SECRET:

When twisting and pulling your twisted cane, be sure to pull the cane next to the flame, not directly in the flame.

Use the "Beach Twist" bead in the "Beach Baby" ring and earrings set, pg. 95.

• Lampwork Artist: Karen Leonardo • Style of Bead: Metallic Bead with Fine Silver Dots •
• Finished Size: 8 mm x 12 mm • Level of Expertise: Beginner •

Metallic Silvered Black

The inspiration for this bead comes from the pure interest of black beads and the fun of using lots of silver. The bead is perfect for contemporary jewelry-makers who use simple, less expensive production beads in their pieces — and every girl loves sparkly jewels!

SUPPLIES:
Effetre Black
Silver reduction frit, size small
1' 28-gauge fine silver wire

TOOLBOX:
Tweezers
Tablespoon for holding frit
Graphite paddle

INSTRUCTIONS:

1. Make a small round bead with the Black glass about 8 mm x 12 mm.

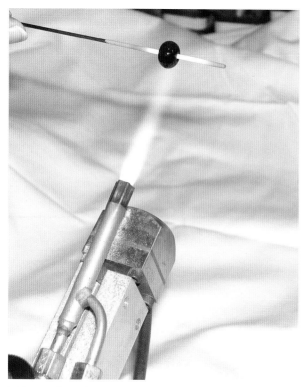

Make a small round.

2. Heat the bead until it is a nice orange glow, and roll it in the silver reduction frit. Be sure the sides of the bead go through the frit. Melt in.

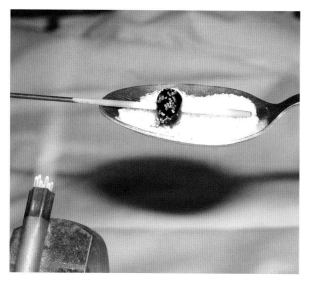

Roll in reduction frit, and melt in.

3. Heat the corner of the bead, and touch the fine silver wire, making it stick to the bead. Wrap the bead in the wire, and heat as you go. End on the other side of the bead, melt off, and push the edges of the wire on with tweezers.

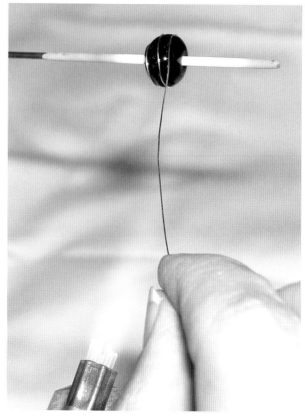

Wrap the bead with fine silver wire.

4. Melt the wire until it beads up. Roll the slightly cool bead over the graphite paddle for the silver dots to stick well.

Melt in and roll on paddle.

5. Flame anneal, and bring out the shine by holding the bead in a reduction flame for a few seconds and turning down the oxygen a bit. You will see the shine "pop" out.

Flame anneal, and bring out the shine of the bead.

HOT GLASS SECRET:

Reduce the glass once, take it out of the flame, and reduce again for a few seconds to bring out the bead's proper shine. If you reduce the bead too long in the flame, you will have a dirty gray finish instead of a shiny metallic gloss.

Use the "Metallic Silver Black" bead in the "High-Sheen Onyx" necklace, pg. 97.

• Lampwork Artist: Karen Leonardo • Style of Bead: Frit Disc •
• Finished Size: 4 mm x 10 mm • Level of Expertise: Beginner •

Metallic Silver Frit Disc

This thin, flat disc bead lies nicely against the round beads and give more interest to any jewelry design. The bumpy edge gives it texture, and the shine makes your piece very noticeable.

SUPPLIES:
Silver reduction frit size #1
Effetre Transparent Light Gray #084

TOOLBOX:
¹⁄₁₆" mandrel
Tablespoon for holding frit
Graphite paddle
Mini mashers

INSTRUCTIONS:

1. Make three small disc beads, about 3 mm x 10 mm.

Make three tiny disc beads.

2. Heat and roll the edge of the discs enough for the silver reduction frit to stick.

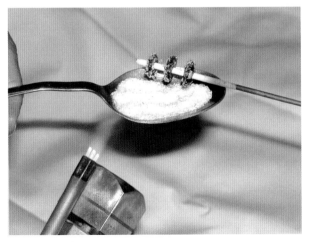

Roll the discs in frit.

3. Straighten the discs by squeezing the sides of the bead with mini mashers, and spin the bead on the graphite paddle to press the frit on the edges.

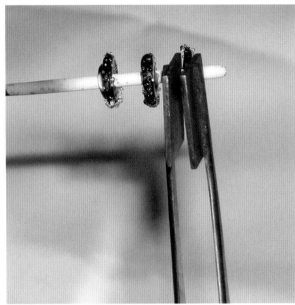

Straighten the discs with mini mashers.

4. Reduce the silver by turning down the oxygen a bit and spinning the disc in the flame for a few seconds. You will see it get shiny in the flame.

Reduce the disc and bring out the silver shine.

HOT GLASS SECRET:

To keep the frit from falling off or breaking off later, heat the very edges of the frit and disc by moving the bead fast near the flame until it has a slight glow. The discs are very heat sensitive since they are so thin. Spin the edges of the disc on the marver to get more frit to stick to the bead. Don't press the disc on the marver, or it may lose its shape; just spin it lightly.

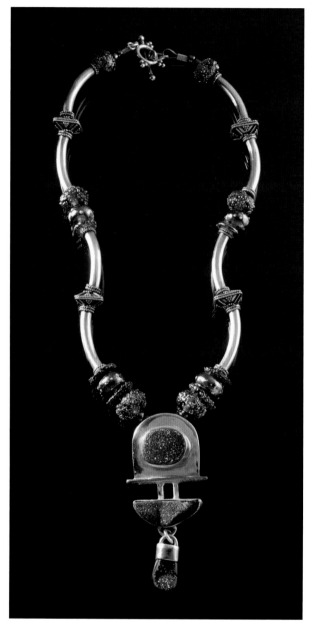

Use the "Metallic Silver Frit Disc" bead in the "High-Sheen Onyx" necklace, pg. 97.

• Lampwork Artist: Bob Leonardo • Style of Bead: Pressed Button •
• Finished Size: 8 mm x 23 mm • Level of Expertise: Beginner •

Bob's Boro

The bead was inspired by walks in the woods admiring creation. There is peace and serenity in a place where you can be alone with Mother Earth, and this bead is a reminder of those special times. You can mold your inspirations into any shape you want with manufactured bead presses. They are fast and uniform, and you have a large canvas from which to work. It would take a long time to freehand your own shape, and some of those shapes would be impossible to make.

SUPPLIES:

Glass Alchemy #385 Silver Strike 5
Glass Alchemy #287 Amazon Bronze
Clear boro

TOOLBOX:

Button bead press*
Graphite paddle
Tweezers

*Used in this project:
Cattwalk bead press

INSTRUCTIONS:

1. Make a base with your Silver Strike to fit the large press.

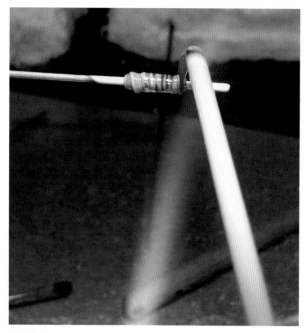

Make a base.

2. Add a stripe of Amazon Bronze down the middle.

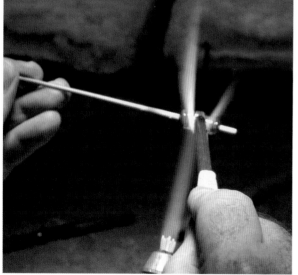

Add a stripe of Amazon Bronze.

3. Measure the base bead to fit the press.

Measure the base to fit your bead.

4. Add a strip of clear to the Silver Strike on both sides, and press. Add more glass to fit the mold, if needed.

5. Add dots of Silver Strike on both sides of the bead.

Add dots of Silver Strike.

6. Heat and press the dots in with your graphite paddle.

Heat and press the dots.

7. Heat and press the shape again in the button press.

Heat and press the bead.

HOT GLASS SECRET:

The best way to determine boro's color reactions is to experiment with a single color and change the flame from reduction to oxidation to see what the color does. If you like a special color, take notes on how you achieved it. There are also tutorials by the glass manufacturers that will give you special recipes on color, and the more you work with the glass, the more you will learn.

8. Fire polish and bring out the colors with a heavy oxidation flame.

Fire polish and bring out the color.

Use "Bob's Boro" in the "Deep Woods" pin, pg. 107.

• Lampwork Artist: Amy Cornett • Style of Bead: Custom Color Encased Disc Bead •
• Finished Size: 5 mm x 15 mm • Level of Expertise: Beginner •

Mixed Color Stack

These beads are perfect with jeans on a casual day; they are simple, elegant and versatile. They are also great with earthy colors and khakis — perfect for a dressed-down day at work.

SUPPLIES:

Effetre Green Pea #212
Effetre Lapis #242
Effetre Brown Dark Red #452
Effetre Periwinkle #220
Effetre Super Clear #006

TOOLBOX:

1/16" mandrels
Parallel press

INSTRUCTIONS:

1. Create custom-mixed denim blue glass by striping a 3" ribbon of the Green Pea, Brown Dark Red and Periwinkle rods to a base rod of Lapis.

Add colors for a custom rod.

2. Begin mixing the colors by working with the base rod. Mix the colors by heating, twisting, pulling and pushing.

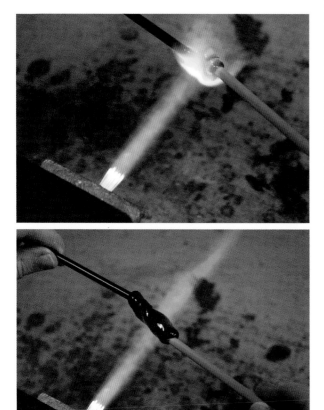

Mix colors.

3. Once the colors are mixed, create a rod by slowly pulling the glass. Set the rod aside to be used once it cools.

Pull custom rod.

4. Using your custom-made denim rod, make a small bead.

Make small bead.

5. Add a layer of clear glass onto the bead to create a disc shape.

Add a layer of clear glass.

6. Heat the encased disc just enough to shape it into a square with the parallel press.

Shape the outer bead into a square.

7. With the parallel press, flatten the sides of the bead for a disc shape.

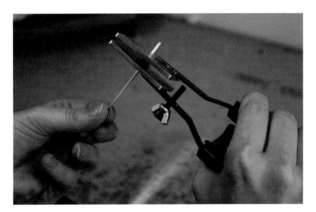

Shape the disc sides.

8. Fire polish to remove the "chill" marks left from the press, by heating just the surface of the bead.

Fire polish and flame anneal.

Use the "Mixed Color Stacks" beads in the "Casual Day" cuff, pg. 118.

HOT GLASS SECRET:

The secret to the custom-made color is to mix the color completely to get a solid new color. You can also mix it partially for a striated look.

HOT GLASS SECRET:

Transparent glass shows everything, so keep your rods clean. Wash your rods often to remove residue from the manufacturer and dust from your studio. Also, remove the cut ends of your rods prior to use by heating and pinching off the tip.

• Lampwork Artist: Karen Leonardo • Style of Bead: Tiny Bright Beads •
• Finished Size: 4 mm x 8 mm • Level of Expertise: Beginner •

Tiny Bright Beach Beads

These tiny beads are perfect for spacers, as dangles on earrings, or in charm bracelets and rings. When you make a handful of them in various colors, the colorful creations will bring a smile to your face.

SUPPLIES:
Effetre Coral #420
Mixed bright-colored frit, size small

TOOLBOX:
Tablespoon to hold frit

INSTRUCTIONS:

1. Make two tiny beads from the Coral.

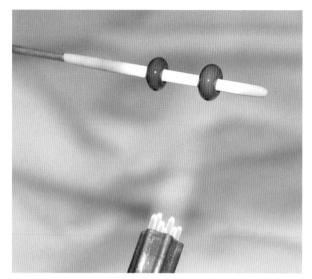

Make two tiny beads.

2. Roll the beads in colored frit. Melt in.

Roll in frit.

Melt in.

3. Flame anneal to finish the beads.

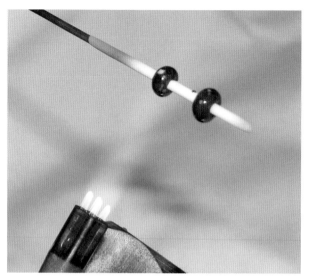

Flame anneal.

Use the "Tiny Bright Beach Bead" in the "Beach Baby" ring and earring set, pg. 95.

HOT GLASS SECRET:

By making two beads on the same mandrel, you can add the same amount of glass to both beads to make a matching pair of earrings.

• Lampworker: Karen Leonardo • Style of bead: Metallic Powder Disc •
• Finished Size: 4 mm x 28 mm, with ⅛" mandrel hole • Level of Expertise: Intermediate •

Archaic Sea Disc

The disc is inspired by the love of the ocean and water. It is a reminder of sunken treasures, similar to coins in a treasure chest that you could find washed up on the beach. The disc is made with various transparent glasses in the colors of the sea with a slight blue and green metallic shine.

SUPPLIES:

Silver Blue reduction powder
Silver Green reduction powder
Aqua Blue reduction frit
Effetre Transparent Medium Aqua #034
Effetre Transparent Light Teal #026
Effetre Transparent Pale Emerald Green #031

TOOLBOX:

3 tablespoons for holding frit and powder
⅛" mandrel with bead release
Graphite paddle
Mini mashers
Bead hole cleaner

INSTRUCTIONS:

1. Make a small, thin donut-shaped bead with the Medium Aqua rod.

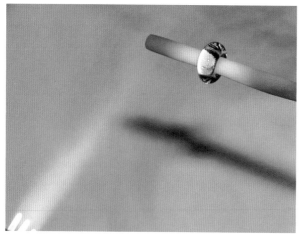

Make a small, thin donut-shaped bead.

2. Roll your bead in the Aqua Blue frit. The bead should be a nice orange so that the frit will stick to it.

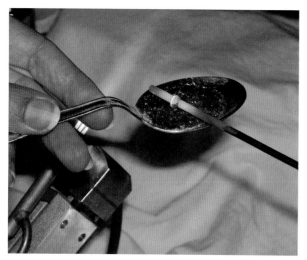

Roll in frit.

HOT GLASS SECRET:

The secret to the making the disc is to make a small base bead and add the glass evenly on top of the next layer Roll fast or spin the disc when heating the bead so it does not become lopsided. The amount of shine depends on how much you reduce the powders.

Once you have the frit on the small bead, heat it in the flame a bit, and roll it on the graphite paddle to help the frit stick a bit more. The frit should not be melted in.

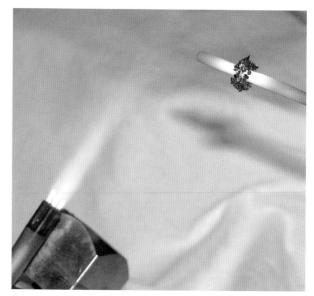

3. Add your second layer of glass by heating enough of the end of the Pale Emerald Green rod to wrap all the way around the bead once. Use an even amount of glass so the disc will be not be lopsided.

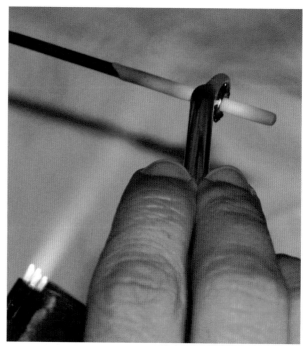

Add a second layer of glass.

Once you have the second layer on, heat that layer only. You will see it go to an orange glow. Do not heat the finished first layer or the bead, or it will melt into one layer or become lopsided. Lightly roll the second layer in the Aqua Blue frit again.

Roll the bead in frit again.

4. Heat in the flame a bit, and roll the edge on the graphite paddle to press the frit on a bit more. If it seems lopsided, use the mini mashers to lightly pinch it straight; the bead has to be warm so you don't crack it with the cool mashers.

5. Add the third layer of the disc using the Light Teal rod. Heat enough of the tip to make another layer that wraps all the way around the bead. Heat just the third layer to an orange glow. Again, use the mini mashers to straighten the bead, or run the graphite paddle along the side to straighten it out as you heat it.

6. Roll and press the Silver Blue powder on the disc.

Roll and press one side in powder.

Heat the disc, and press one edge of the disc into the Silver Blue powder in various areas, leaving a bit of the disc showing. Repeat this with the other side of the disc, and then roll the outer edge in it. Repeat with the Silver Green powder.

7. Reduce the disc to give it the metallic finish. The amount of metallic finish you get will depend on how long you roll the bead in the flame. Use a slight reduction flame by turning down the oxygen a bit. Roll the sides of the bead in the flame for about three seconds on each side and the edge of the disc. If you prefer a more metallic-looking finish, reduce again — but be careful not to over-reduce the disc, or it will turn a dull, gray color.

Reduce the disc.

Use the "Archaic Sea Disc" bead in the "Santorini Fossils" choker, pg. 114.

• Lampwork Artist: Lezlie Belanger • Style of Bead: Sculpted Sheep Bead •
• Finished Size: 14 mm x 16 mm x 20 mm • Level of Expertise: Intermediate •

Have You Any Wool?

This sculpted bead was inspired by the many children's stories and nursery rhymes that we still enjoy today. Do you remember the rhyme, "Baa baa black sheep have you any wool?" Bring back any memories yet?

SUPPLIES:

Effetre White P-204
Effetre Black T-064
Effetre Coral S-420
Effetre White P-204 stringer

TOOLBOX:

Exacto knife
Parallel mashers
Tweezer mashers
Pointed tweezers

INSTRUCTIONS:

1. Start by winding the White glass on a lemon-shaped base.

Wind the glass.

2. Heat the lemon shape, and let the glass sag a little to the bottom of the mandrel to add more weight to the bottom of the sheep. Balance is important. You want more glass on the bottom side of the bead so that your sheep will remain upright in your jewelry design instead of flipping upside-down.

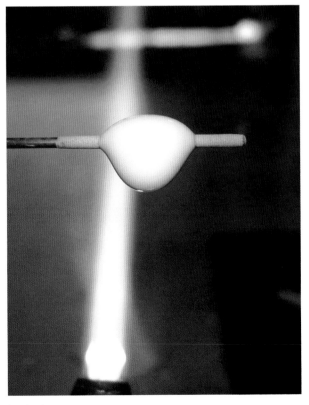

Let the glass sag.

3. Flatten the lemon shape with the parallel mashers or tweezers.

Flatten the shape.

4. Add dots of Black for the legs and tail; this is just to establish the location, so you can add more glass later to adjust the size. Add a fairly large dot of White where the face will be.

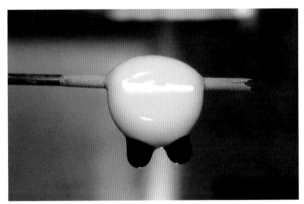

Add black dots for legs.

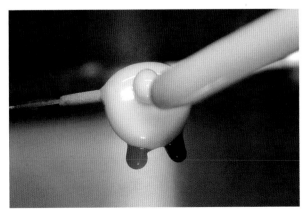

Add a large white dot for the face.

5. Now it's time to add lots of dots to make your sheep fluffy. I use a pre-made stringer for this, but you can pull your own if you prefer. Begin at the legs and work up, trying for a random look. Cover the whole sheep except for the face, legs and tail.

Add small dots for fluffy wool.

6. Shape the face by squeezing gently with tweezers to make the face longer than it is wide, and nudge it down gently against the body of the sheep. You don't want it to protrude too far out from the body.

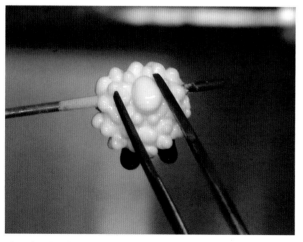

Shape head with tweezers.

7. Add a small dot for the ears at the upper sides of the face, and press them with pointy tweezers to shape. Turn the bead, and gently press the tail. Crease it slightly with an exacto blade.

Add black dots and shape ears.

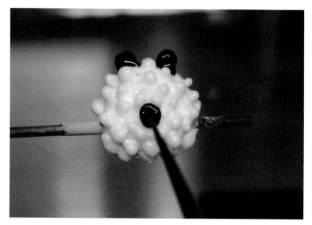

Shape the tail.

HOT GLASS SECRET:

The secret to making this bead is placing the dots to look like wool and controlling your heat in the bead as you work to keep the dots or "wool" from melting too much.

8. Now, add tiny dots of black for the eyes, and add tiny dots of white for the fluff on the top of the head between the ears (this is tricky; you want to melt them in just enough to attach firmly, but not too much or they'll melt into one shapeless blob).

Add small white dots to top of head.

Add tiny black dots for eyes.

9. Add the dot for the nose; Coral works best, but pink is also a good choice.

Add a coral dot for the nose.

10. Heat the whole bead in the upper part of the flame to even out the heat base, and then place the bead in your kiln to anneal.

Use the "Have You Any Wool?" bead in the "Baabs" necklace, pg. 93.

• Lampwork Artist: Lezlie Belanger/Canterbury Keepsakes • Style of Bead: Encased Implosion Round Bead •
• Finished Size: approx. 14 mm round • Level of Expertise: Intermediate •

Lilypad

This feminine bead was inspired by the serenity and beauty of water lilies in a pond. The colors can vary like those in a tranquil fragrant garden. It's exciting to watch the dots turn into lily petals. If only they smelled as pretty as they look!

MATERIALS:
Effetre Clear
Effetre stringer in opaque colors

TOOLBOX:
No extra tools required

INSTRUCTIONS:

1. Make a thin flat disk with the clear glass.

Make a clear glass disc.

2. Lay down a circle of dots on the bead, close to the mandrel. Heat the whole disk, and then lay down another circle of dots. Space them so they are between the dots in the previous circle. Make sure they don't touch each other, and make sure that there's a little clear showing between each dot.

Place the dots.

3. Continue heating, and add another circle of dots until you have at least three circles. You can add more, depending on the effect you want to create. Larger, fewer dots and fewer layers will make a thicker, wider flower petal; more dots and layers will make a thinner petal.

> ## HOT GLASS SECRET:
> The secret to making this bead is the proper use of gravity to pull the clear glass over the dots and allow the dots to form flower petals.

4. Now comes the tricky part! Carefully melt in the dots, concentrating the heat on the inside of the disk at first near the mandrel, and working out to heat the outer edge of the disk. Don't let the disk get too hot, or it will get floppy and start melting unevenly, distorting your petal design.

Melt in dots.

5. As you heat it, the disk will begin to draw in toward the mandrel. Let gravity and the heat pull the clear glass over the dots.

Let gravity pull the clear glass over the dots.

6. You'll see the flower petals taking shape and lengthening as the disk melts. You can change the way the flower looks by tilting the mandrel and letting gravity move the glass down the mandrel, either towards the bottom side of the flower for a more open flower shape, or toward the top on the flower for a longer, leaner flower with thinner petals.

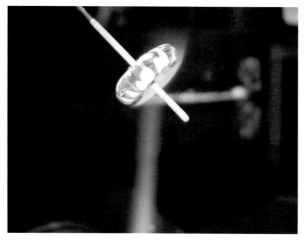

Flower petals will appear.

Finished bead.

Use the "Lilypad" bead in the "Pond and Sea" necklace, pg. 102.

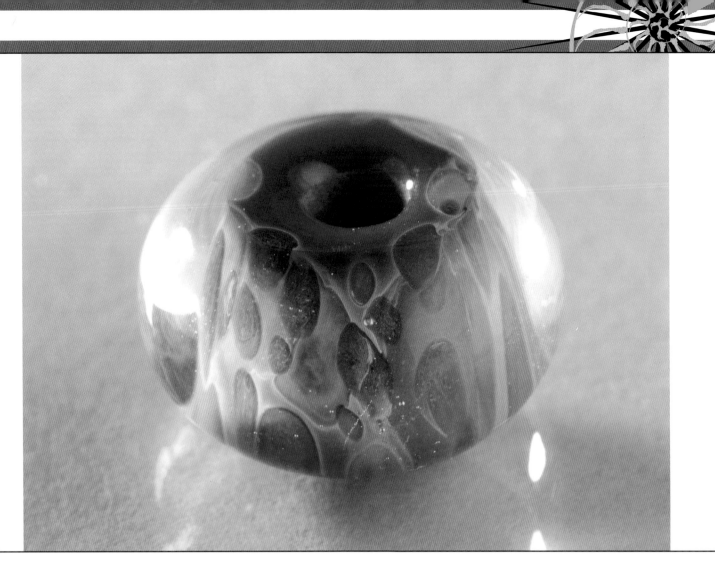

• Lampwork Artist: Leslie Kaplan • Style of Bead: Encased Boro Frit Bead •
• Finished Size: 9 mm x 14 mm • Level of Expertise: Intermediate •

Midst of the Garden

The bead was inspired by the lovely array of muted colors in a garden: greens, purples, yellows and blues. The borosilicate glass allows the colors to mix and transfer a glow as if the sun were shining. The clear encasement of the frits magnifies the color, and the type of flame you use changes the colors of your lovely garden. No gardening tools needed here — just your torch and supplies!

SUPPLIES:

Northstar 73 – Millenium Moss
Glass Alchemy 486 – Peacock Chameleon
New Color (Roger Paramore) – Sage
Precision – Crystal Bliss
Northstar 53 – Forest Green
Glass Alchemy 559 – Neptune Sparkle
Simax clear borosilicate
Glass Alchemy 385 Frit – Silver Strike 5, size 1
Glass Alchemy 487 Frit – Amazon Jewel, size 2

TOOLBOX:

Boroscopes
Graphite pad

INSTRUCTIONS:

PREPARE:

Pile a generous amount of Silver Strike 5 and smaller Amazon Jewel frit on a graphite pad. Place the frits near the torch on the side of your dominant hand.

Prepare the frits.

MAKE THE BEAD:

1. Make a small bead with Forest Green.

Make a small bead.

2. Bring the bead up to a bright glow, and then roll the bead in the Silver Strike 5 large frit. Melt in.

Roll in Silver Strike 5.

3. Bring the bead up to a bright glow, and then roll the bead in the Amazon Jewel frit.

Roll the bead in Amazon Jewel.

4. Melt the frit into the surface of the bead until it is smooth and even again.

Melt in the frit.

5. Encase the bead with clear glass. Keep the bead warm, but not hot. Heat up an inch of the clear boro rod to cover the bead with the clear as evenly as possible. Overlap the ends or go around the bead twice. Add a little more clear if the coverage does not seem even or if your bead is lopsided.

Add clear glass.

6. Heat the bead until the clear glass melts evenly onto the surface.

Melt in.

You can direct the heat at the ends of the bead if the clear is not covering them adequately. The glass will flow toward the heat.

7. If you want some pink/purple tones in this bead, strike it. (If not, place the bead into the kiln now.) To strike, remove the bead from the flame until you can see that the orange glow is gone.

Remove the beads for a few seconds.

Strike colors by rotating the bead in the upper portion of the flame.

8. Put the bead back in the cooler upper portion of the flame, 6"–8" from the torch head. Rotate the bead slowly until it has a dull orange glow. Continue rotating for 20 seconds or so, then put the bead in the kiln.

HOT GLASS SECRET:

The secret to maintaining continuity of color in the frit bead is to use the same size and type of flame (measured by the oxygen and propane ratio).

Use "Midst of the Garden" beads in the "Growing Things" bracelet, pg. 126.

SAFETY TIP:

Eye protection is very important. If you work with Borosilicate glass, don't rely on didymium lenses (soft glass lenses). Instead, use additional protection like a boroscope or a #4 welding shade.

• Lampwork Artist: Christine Schneider • Style of Bead: Encased Round Bubble Bead •
• Finished Size: 8 mm x 12 mm • Level of Expertise: Intermediate •

Night Has A Thousand Eyes

This bead reflects the moonlit colors and has a textured surface to bring tactile interest to the wearer. The "Night" colors are very soft and gentle. Imagine the moon shining on a red car — what do you see? Certainly not red! Instead, the car is a muted purple or blue.

SUPPLIES:

Effetre Transparent Dark Lavender T-081
Effetre Transparent Ink Blue T-058
Effetre Transparent Pale Emerald Green T-031
Effetre Transparent Sage Green T-019
Effetre Opaque White P-204
Effetre Transparent Clear T-004

TOOLBOX:

3/32" tungsten poker
Tweezers
Pliers

INSTRUCTIONS:

1. Pull a 2 mm or smaller stringer from both the Sage Green and Ink Blue rods, and set aside.

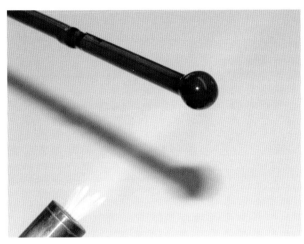

Pull stringers from the two rods.

2. Create a very small white glass bead, 6 mm or smaller.

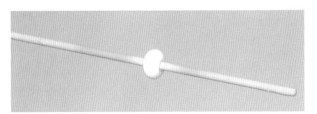

Make a small white bead.

3. Encase the white bead (the base) with Pale Emerald by using two wraps of glass over the middle of the white. Melt in.

Encase the white bead.

4. Place five evenly spaced white dots around your bead. Leave these dots raised.

Place five white dots.

5. Place dots of Dark Lavender on top of the white dots.

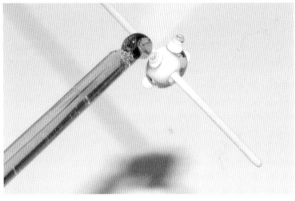

Place dark lavender dots.

6. Gently melt the dots in. This will give you the basis for your pattern.

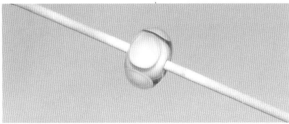

Melt in dots.

HOT GLASS SECRET:

Make this bead using little trapped air bubbles strategically placed to fascinate those who wonder how they got there.

7. Using the Ink Blue stringer you made in Step 1, place tiny dots in the center of your larger dots, and melt them flat.

Add ink blue dots.

8. Allow your bead to firm up at this stage. Then, using your tungsten poker, warm each of the dots on the bead individually, and poke into the center to create a small dent. Don't heat the poker before doing this — it only works if the poker is cooler then the glass.

Poke the dots.

Use the "Night Has a Thousand Eyes" bead in the bracelet, pg. 111.

9. Over each of the dents you created, place a tiny bit of clear glass. Be careful to cover the entire dent so that the air bubble can't escape.

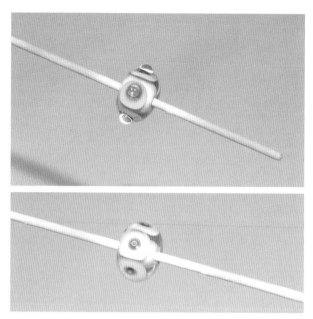

Add clear dots over hole.

10. Using the Sage Green stringer you made in the beginning, begin placing your tiny raised dots evenly on the bead. Let the dots melt in just slightly, flame anneal and put in the kiln.

Place tiny raised dots with the Sage Green stringer.

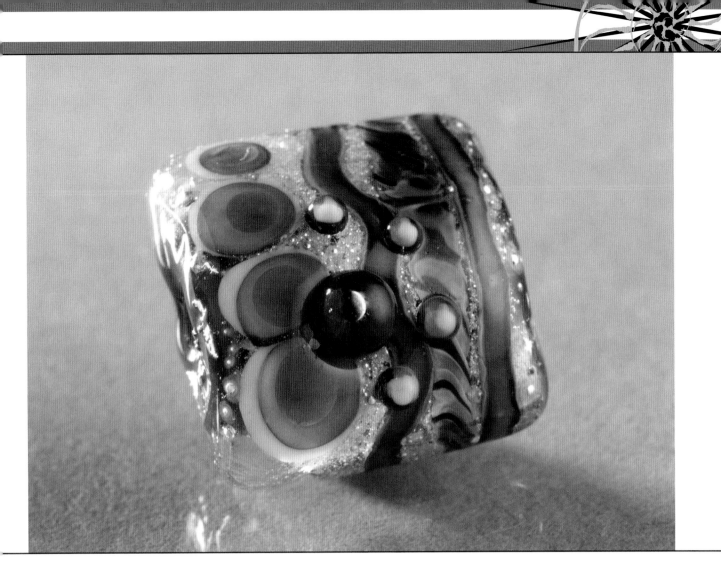

• Lampwork Artist: Sue Booth • Style of Bead: Silver Leaf and Raku Pillow Bead •
• Finished Size: 15 mm x 16 mm • Level of Expertise: Advanced •

Autumn Glow

The beautiful Autumn Glow bead has fall-inspired colors with a hint of sparkle, thanks to pure silver. The Raku 'starburst' murrini and latticino add just the right amount of interest to this bead. The pressed shape allows for a sleek fit and a nicely sized canvas to decorate for a small bead. These beautiful beads are perfect for a bracelet or earrings.

SUPPLIES:

Effetre Transparent Dark Amber T-016
Effetre Transparent Pale Amber T-012
Effetre Opal Yellow P-266
Effetre Black T-064
Effetre Metallic Silver Plum P-275
Effetre White P-204
Reichenbach Iris Orange (Raku) RW-108
Vetrofond Clear V-004
¼ sheet silver foil 99.9% silver content

TOOLBOX:

Uncoated ³⁄₃₂" mandrels (to prepare cane)
Pliers or tweezers
Small glass mashers
Glass rod nippers
Plunging tool/tungsten pick
Cattwalk Sleek Pillow Press
Graphite marver or paddle

INSTRUCTIONS:

MURRINI STRINGER:

1. Melt a small pea-sized blob of Black glass, and pull it into a medium-sized stringer. Put aside.

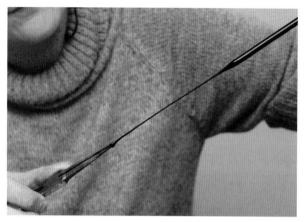

Make Black Stringer, set aside.

2. Wind a small disk of Reichenbach Iris Orange on the end of an uncoated ³⁄₃₂" mandrel.

Make a small disc of raku.

3. Hold the mandrel at a 45-degree angle. Aim the flame at the disk until it starts to ball up and form a teardrop shape.

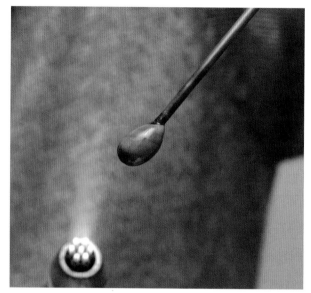

Melt into a teardrop shape.

4. Center the glass on the mandrel using small glass mashers.

Center the glass.

HOT GLASS SECRET:

To achieve the best colors from the raku latticino, super-heat the latticino. When you see a "white-orange" glow to your latticino and it starts to spread out on the surface of your bead, immediately take it out of the flame and gently marver or shape the latticino into the bead.

5. Using the Black stringer you made earlier, paint on six to eight lines.

Paint six to eight black lines.

6. Melt in.

Melt in.

7. Heat the glass. Slowly pull gather until it has reached the desired thickness. Cut the murrini stringer from the end of the mandrel with the rod nippers. Set aside.

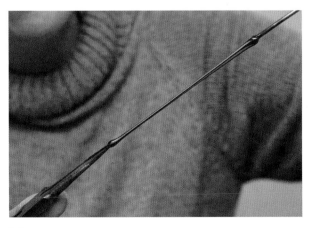

Pull cane.

ENCASED DARK AMBER STRINGER:

1. Wind a small disk of White glass on the end of an uncoated ³⁄₃₂" mandrel.

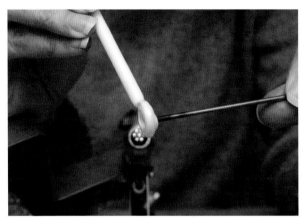

Make a small ball of white glass.

2. Hold the mandrel at a 45-degree angle. Aim the flame at the disk until it starts to ball up. Form a cylinder shape using the graphite paddle.

Form a cylinder shape.

3. Using the Transparent Dark Amber, wrap the White core completely.

Wrap the White core with Dark Amber.

4. Melt in, and marver to keep the shape.

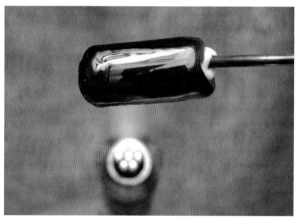

Melt in and shape.

5. Slowly heat the glass until it is glowing but not too molten. Remove from the flame, and wait a few seconds until a "skin" starts to form. Slowly pull the glass with your pliers until you achieve the desired thickness of your stringer. Cut a stringer off the rod with rod nippers. Set aside.

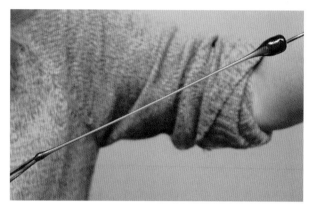

Pull a stringer.

RAKU LATTICINO:

1. Wind a small disk of Black glass on the end of an uncoated ³⁄₃₂" mandrel.

Wind a black disc.

2. Melt in, and form a teardrop shape.

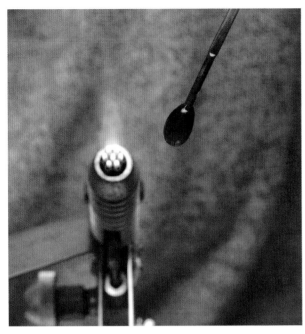

Form a teardrop shape.

3. Squeeze flat with glass mashers into a paddle shape.

Flatten the glass.

4. Paint two stripes of Reichenbach Iris Orange on both sides of the paddle. Melt in. Maintain the paddle shape.

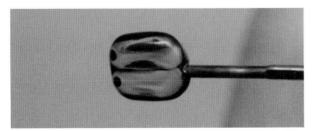

Stripe on the raku.

5. Encase the paddle with Clear glass.

Encase with clear glass.

6. Super-heat the tip of an uncoated mandrel. Plunge the mandrel into the glass.

Attach the mandrel.

7. Heat the glass until molten but not drippy. Take the glass out of the flame, and wait until a "skin" forms (about three or four seconds). Then, pull while twisting your hands in opposite directions.

Melt, pull and twist.

AUTUMN GLOW BEAD:

1. Lay aside ¼ sheet of silver foil.

2. Wind a small barrel of Transparent Dark Amber.

Make a small barrel.

3. Make sure the barrel is a few millimeters shy of each side of the cavity of your pillow press.

Measure the barrel in the press

4. Using a rod of Clear glass, encase the barrel.

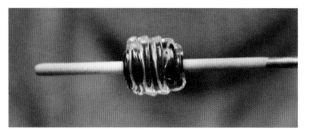

Encase the barrel in clear glass.

5. Melt the encasing.

Melt in.

6. Roll your slightly warm (but not molten) bead in silver foil, and press the foil into the surface of the bead with your graphite paddle.

Wrap and press silver on the bead.

7. Introduce the bead back into the flame. Burn off the residual silver foil, and melt in.

Melt in the silver foil.

8. Reheat your bead until warm but not fully molten, and place it in the cavity of your pillow press. Press straight down.

Press in the pillow press.

9. If you've added a little too much glass, your bead may look a little uneven. If so, all you need do is straighten it up by gently heating each edge and pushing it up with your graphite paddle.

Straighten up the end.

10. Apply the raku latticino to the left side of the bead. Keep the bead right underneath the flame as you go through the flame, slightly pressing the latticino on the bead.

Apply the raku latticino.

11. Gently marver the latticino into the bead.

Marver the raku latticino.

12. Place four dots of Opal Yellow on both sides of the bead. Melt in.

Place four dots of Opal Yellow.

13. Place a dot of Pale Amber on top of each dot of the Opal Yellow. Add a tiny dot of Transparent Dark Amber on top of the Pale Amber.

Place four dots of Pale Amber and Dark Amber.

14. Add random designs on either side of the raku latticino, using your encased Dark Amber stringer.

Place a random stringer design on the bead.

15. Melt all the designs into the surface of the bead.

Melt all designs into the bead.

16. Super-heat a spot on one side of your bead.

Super-heat one side of the bead.

17. Plunge the tip of the murrini stringer into the super-heated spot. Once the cane is firmly positioned, cut the glass off with the rod nipper, leaving three or four millimeters of cane above the surface of the bead.

Plunge the murrini cane into the bead.

18. Repeat this process on the other side of your bead.

Repeat on the other side.

19. Heat the murrini, grab your tungsten pick or plunging tool, and plunge it into the center of the murrini so you form a starburst pattern. Repeat on the other side of your bead. Leave slightly raised.

Plunge a tungsten pick into the heated murrini.

20. Add a tiny drop of clear on top of each murrini to help lock in the colors and magnify the murrini.

Add a tiny dot of clear glass.

21. Using your encased Dark Amber stringer, apply random dots on both sides of your bead around the raku murrini.

Apply dots of encased Dark Amber stringer.

22. Flame anneal your bead in the upper portion of the flame, making sure that it is evenly heated, and place the bead in your kiln.

Flame anneal.

Use the "Autumn Glow" bead in the "African Cat Trail" bracelet, pg. 104.

• Lampwork artist: JC Herrell • Style of Bead: Kronos Flat Tab •
• Finished Size: 12 mm wide x 45 mm tall x 41 mm across • Level of Expertise: Advanced •

Fire and Ice Flow Bead

The bead has a dark red base, which is inspired by the flow of lava. The bits of silver gray come from the "ashes" and steam as the lava flow hits the blue "kronos" waters. The flat tab is a bead that lays nicely against the skin, and the large size of the bead says, "look at me!"

SUPPLIES:

4"–6" of Kronos rod from Double Helix
1–3 rods Effetre T-076 Transparent Red

TOOLBOX:

2 graphite paddles (or parallel mashers)
Tweezers or pliers (for pulling stringer)
Butter knife
Osibin Lentil Shaper
Small diameter mandrel, pre-dipped
in strong bead release

INSTRUCTIONS:

1. Pull a few stringers from your rod of Kronos. You will need three or four stringers that are about 2½–3 feet long and 2 mm–3 mm wide. A thicker stringer is better than a thin stringer for this application.

When gathering a ball of molten glass to pull into the stringer, be sure to use plenty of oxygen in your flame.

If you experience hazing, turn down the propane on your torch. Hazing is a grayish-white scum that builds up on the bead if you use certain colors. Remove haze by turning down the propane and heating the bead in an oxygen-rich flame.

2. Lay down the base, or footprint, of your bead with the Transparent Red, approximately 35 mm–38 mm long.

Make a base.

3. Add more glass to your bead until you have an oval shape, bring it to an even and flowing hot state. Take the bead in and out of the flame now and then for the bead to process heat inward. If you don't allow the bead to process heat, it will be hard to press your shape.

Add heat.

4. Let the bead cool until it only has a calm inner glow, and then shape the bead into a rough football shape. Heat just two thirds of the bead until it is glowing red and easily shapeable.

Heat two thirds of the bead.

5. Use the lentil shaper to gently shape the bead into a nice, tapered cone on the heated side. You may have to heat and shape a few times to make it even.

Shape one side.

6. Heat the other side of the bead.

Heat the other two thirds of the bead.

7. Again, use the lentil shaper to gently shape the bead into a nice, tapered cone on the other side. Reheat and reshape this side a few times to make it even.

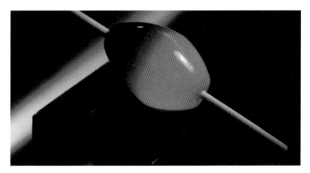

Shape the second side.

8. Stripe the stringer along the length of the bead at regular intervals until you have come back around to your first line. Remember, the look is organic so nothing needs to be done too precisely! Always be sure to keep your flame rich in oxygen (pretty hot) when working the bead after the stringer is applied. The hot, oxygenated flame will prevent the haze from forming before you are ready.

Stripe the bead with the stringer.

9. Heat each end of the bead to bring the stringer together.

Heat each end.

10. Heat the middle to melt the stringer in most of the way.

Heat the middle.

11. Apply more stringer to fill in the gaps of the stripes you just created.

Apply more stringer.

12. After covering rest of the bead with stringer, heat one end of the bead to allow the stringer stripes to flow together and cover the end of the bead. Do the same to the other side of the bead.

Heat one end.

13. If you have a large, off-center mass, try shaping it into place with a butter knife or shaper while the bead is still molten. Then, reheat and re-center.

Shape the ends of the bead with a knife.

14. If needed, shape the end with the lentil shaper again to retain an oval shape.

Reshape with the lentil shaper.

15. Evenly heat the bead to a red-hot glow so that it is molten and mushy.

Evenly heat the bead.

16. When the bead is molten hot, remove it from the flame. While continuing to rotate the bead, wait a couple of seconds for the heat to even out within the bead (remember that time out of the flame is as important as time in the flame). Use this time to evaluate the patterns that have formed and decide where you would like the front and back of the bead. When the glow has settled and the bead has had a chance to bring the heat to its core, it is time to flatten the bead into a tab shape. Press the bead between the two graphite paddles with a smooth, even, slow squeeze. If it is not flat enough, reheat and flatten the bead some more.

Flatten the bead between the graphite paddles.

17. Fire polish the surface of the bead. Turn the oxygen way up, and burn off any extra hazing in the red that peeks through the stringer. The red is very vulnerable to fuming from the silver in the stringer, and it tends to haze up easily. This is something you can choose to take advantage of or try to diminish, depending on the effect you want.

Fire polish the bead.

18. After fire polishing both sides, let the bead cool until it loses all of its glow. Introduce it into a light reduction flame with either reduced oxygen or increased propane. Some of the best reactions happen right at the tip of the candle (the pointy bright orange flame within the larger blue flame). Soak one side of the bead in the reduction flame for a few seconds; you will notice some haze and color starting to develop. Remove the bead from the flame, and let it cool before repeating the step on the second side. Be aware of the heat level and softness of the bead, because you don't want to lose the shape and have to re-press the bead. Repeat this step until you are happy with the haze and color that has formed on the bead. The color forms as the surface glass of the Kronos glass transitions from a relatively cool temperature into a warmer one in the right flame chemistry. The reduction flame and where you hold the bead is just as important as the cooling and heating of the glass.

19. This last step is optional. If you want to remove some of the haze and/or metallic lusters that can develop in the reduction flame, use a pinpoint oxygen-rich flame to polish the bead and finesse the colors.

Optional polish.

Reduce the bead.

Use the "Fire and Ice" bead in the "Moon Shadow" bracelet, pg. 129.

HOT GLASS SECRET:

You'll notice a border of ivory or charcoal develop between the Kronos and Transparent Red. This will happen as a reaction occurs between the two colors. You can keep this to a minimum by continuing to use an oxygen-rich flame but you cannot eliminate it. Some people really like a strong "charcoal" effect, and you can use a slightly reducing flame to bring this out more.

SAFETY TIP:

Double Helix glass and other popular reacting colors are rich in metals! Be aware that these metals tend to vaporize during use. Please take appropriate precautions and adequate forced air ventilation when using these colors.

• Lampwork Artist: Cindy Palmer • Style of Bead: Reichenbach Bicone •
• Finished Size: 40 mm x 20 mm • Level of Expertise: Advanced •

Luscious Pink Mosaic

Reichenbach glass has deep, vibrant colors, and the bicone shape has a wonderful sleek, long look. When you heat the glass and push the colors against each other, they create beautiful lines of crispness that you see in the grout lines of mosaics. What inspiration!

SUPPLIES:

Effetre White 204
Effetre Transparent Black 064
Reichenbach Iris Orange Opaque R108-C (Raku)
Reichenbach Heliotrope Transparent R11-C
Reichenbach Turquoise Transparent R49-C

TOOLBOX:

Osibin Lentil Shaper
Tweezers

INSTRUCTIONS:

1. Pull 1 mm–2 mm stringers of Heliotrope and Turquoise, as well as 3 mm–4 mm stringers of Black and Iris Orange.

2. Wind a large footprint onto the mandrel using white, (the footprint should be approximately 37 mm from end to end). Continue to add glass to the bead until you have about a 20 mm–thick bead. Melt in all of your glass.

Make the base bead.

3. Heat the bead to a full red glow, and shape the bead into a soft bicone using the lentil shaper.

Heat and shape

4. Using your 1 mm–2 mm stringer of Heliotrope, place three or four horizontal lines on the bead. Two of the lines should go from end to end, and the other lines can stop partway through the bead (this leaves space for dots).

Add heliotrope lines.

5. Add Turquoise lines using your 1 mm–2 mm stringer the same way you added Heliotrope in Step 4.

Add turquoise lines.

6. Thoroughly heat all of the lines, and be certain that they are fused to your base bead without losing the shape of your base bead. You don't want them to come loose when you proceed to the next step.

Heat the lines, and fuse the lines to the ends.

7. Using your 3 mm–4 mm stringers, place dots of Heliotrope, Turquoise and Black in the white spaces of your base bead. Leave about a dot's width between your dots.

Add dots.

HOT GLASS SECRET:

Reichenbach glass is expensive and highly concentrated. It is better used as a stringer or as a thin layer applied over a soft glass base to be more economical and spread the color out.

8. Melt in all of the lines and dots you have placed, while keeping your base bead shape. Be sure to concentrate heat on the ends of your bead as well as the center of the bead. This ensures that your design will go from one end to the other end of your bead and not get sucked toward the middle. To do this, focus the flame directly on the end of the bead, aiming straight through the mandrel. This will pull your lines and dots toward the mandrel so that your design will truly go to the end of the bead.

Melt all lines and dots in.

9. Place raku dots on the transparent black dots you placed earlier. The black dots should be only slightly larger than the raku dots.

Add raku dots over the black dots; melt in.

10. Thoroughly heat your bead, making sure not to distort your base bead. Next, focus the flame on the right end of your bead. Heat one end of the bead (about one third) until it is red-hot, and let the glass flow around the mandrel, rotating the mandrel when the glass starts to droop. Let it droop again, and rotate once more. Continue letting the glass droop and rotating the mandrel until you have beautiful marbling around the bead.

Heat the bead to flowing.

11. Re-shape the hot end of the bead to a soft bicone using your lentil shaper.

Shape the hot end.

12. Repeat Steps 10 and 11 on the left side of your bead.

Repeat on the other side of bead.

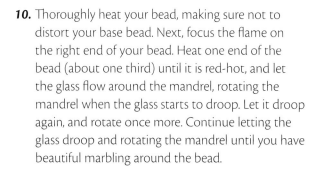

13. Heat and fire polish the entire bead. Flame anneal. Place the bead in the kiln.

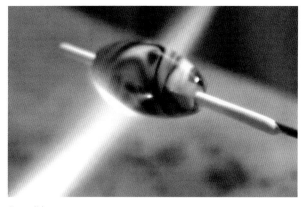

Fire polish.

Use the "Luscious Pink Mosaic" bead in the "Hot Spanish Days" necklace, pg. 99.

• Lampwork Artist: Cathy Lybarger • Style of Bead: Mask Bead with Eye Murrini •
• Finished Size: 52 mm x 26 mm x 21 mm • Level of Expertise: Advanced •

Mango Nymph

The inspiration for this mask bead came from the love of things that are wild and crazy. Our world is all about color! The masks show contrasting colors, bright colors and crazy colors! What would life be without beautiful, bold color? It just puts a smile on your face!

SUPPLIES:

Effetre Dark Yellow 412
Effetre Dark Turquoise 236
Effetre Light Turquoise 232
Effetre Transparent Dark Emerald Green 030
Effetre Periwinkle 220
Effetre Transparent Cobalt Blue 060
Effetre Red Orange 428
Effetre Intense Black 066
Effetre Petroleum Green 218
Effetre White 204
Effetre Clear 004
Effetre Coral 420

TOOLBOX:

3" x 4" graphite paddle
Parallel mashers
Tweezers
Utility blade or Exacto knife

73

INSTRUCTIONS:

THE STRINGER:

1. Encase about 1" of the White rod with Cobalt. This amount of glass should be good for two short pulls of thick stringer.

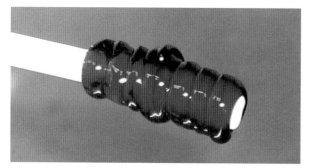

Wrap the core.

2. Heat about half of the encased area until it glows orange. Remove it from the flame, and grasp a small amount at the end with a tweezers. Wait a few seconds for the glass to cool before pulling, and then pull slowly. This will ensure that you will get a good, thick stringer.

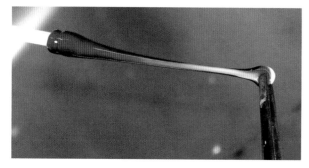

Pull a thick stringer.

3. Burn off the first stringer.

Burn off the end.

4. Pull a second stringer.

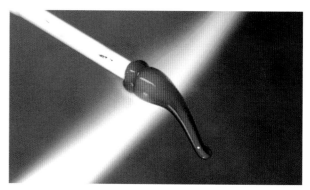

Pull second stringer.

5. Melt off where the Cobalt meets the White rod.

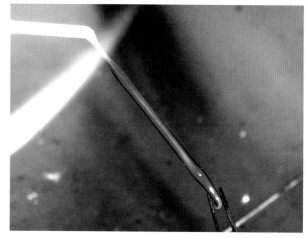

Burn off the stringer.

6. Repeat Steps 1–8, using the Transparent Dark Emerald over White.

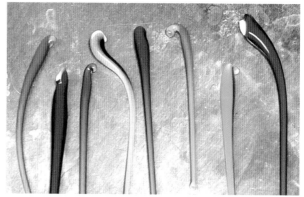

Make more stringers.

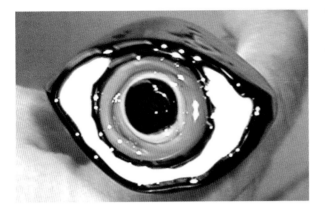

SUPPLIES FOR EYEBALL MURRINI:

3 10 mm Clear borosilicate punties (2 with slightly flattened ends, and 1 with a slightly pointed end)

Effetre White

Effetre Nile Green

Effetre Grass Green

Effetre 8 mm–10 mm Intense black

Effetre 5 mm–6 mm Clear

8 Intense Black stringers, 2 mm

5 Clear stringers, 2 mm

TOOLBOX:

3" x 4" hand-held graphite paddle (or other marver)

Rod lopper

Tweezers

HOT GLASS SECRET:

The object of this project is to pull an uneven cane. A cane of varying thickness will assure you a variety of eyeball sizes for your mask beads. This recipe should yield about 11"–12" of eyeball cane ranging from 6 mm x 10 mm to 11 mm x 15 mm.

You may also cut smaller diameter cane with a rod lopper. For best results, your murrini chips should be very thin (about 3 mm). Murrini cane in the 11 mm to 15 mm range (usually closer to the ends of the cane) may need to be cut with a diamond band saw in order to make nice, flat slices.

THE EYEBALL MURRINI:

1. Turn on your kiln. Heat kiln to temperature (to add eye cane when completed). Preheat the 8 mm–10 mm Intense Black rod. This rod will be the pupil of the eye. Encase 1" of the end of the rod with Nile Green. (Keeping your gather at one inch or just slightly larger will help keep your glass a manageable size.) The Nile Green will be the first layer of the iris in your eye. Place a layer of a lighter color next to the pupil — it will give the eye more depth. Be sure to wind the glass around the rod rather than striping up and down, because striping can leave undesirable dents around your pupil. Be sure to keep the green very hot while holding the black beneath your flame. If the black heats up and bends, simply remove it from the flame and straighten it using a graphite paddle.

Smooth out the ridges in your first layer of Nile Green by heating the gather and rolling it on a marver. Make sure all of the gaps in the green glass are filled before continuing.

Make a smooth layer.

2. When the Nile Green layer is smooth and free of bubbles, begin winding the Grass Green around it. When the first layer of Grass Green is smooth, apply a second layer. This should complete the iris (colored part) of your eye. Marver the three layers so they are smooth and bubble-free.

Marver the three layers.

3. As your gather gets larger and heavier, the Intense Black rod will become more and more likely to crack — so at this point, attach a borosilicate punty and burn off the Intense Black rod. Use the slightly pointed (like a pencil) punty for this step; since the pointed shape holds less surface area, it will be easier to remove later on.

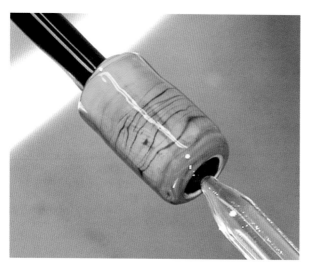

Attach the pointed punty.

4. Wind a layer of Intense Black stringer all the way around your iris. It is important that it is thin and uniform.

Wind black stringer.

5. Next, build the white area around the iris. The white will not go all the way around the iris, so stripe the glass down the gather rather than winding it all the way around the bead. Begin by making two stripes about ¼" to ½" apart, depending on the size of your eye. Fill in everything but that ¼" to ½" gap with White. Marver the gather to round it out.

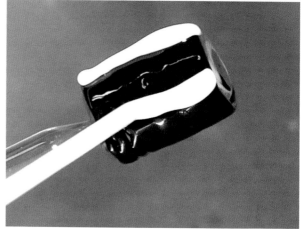

Lay down white stripes.

6. Build up the white on either side of the eye, and marver it into a football shape.

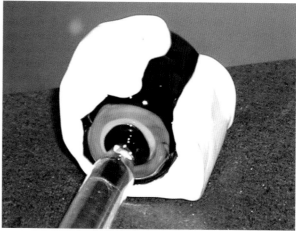

Build and marver.

7. Coat the entire circumference of your football-shaped eye (or murrini bundle) with Intense Black stringer. Marver it smooth.

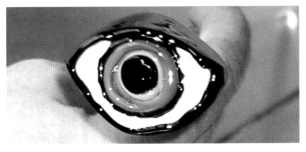

Finish the eye.

8. Next, coat the circumference with Clear stringer. The clear layer will keep the Intense Black from feathering out onto your base color.

Coat with clear stringer.

9. Heat and flatten the unpuntied end of your murrini bundle against your marver. This will prevent bubbles from forming when you encase the end in Clear.

10. Encase the end of the eye using the 5 mm–6 mm Clear rod. Continue to add glass until you form a dome of clear glass at the end. The clear dome keeps you from pulling on and distorting your bundle.

Encase the eye in a clear cone.

11. Attach a flat-ended borosilicate punty to the domed end of your bundle. Heat both the bundle and the punty before sticking them together.

12. Remove the pointed punty from the other end of the bundle by tapping it against your torch head. It should pop right off, but if it does not, hold it out of the flame for a moment or two and try tapping again. Be sure to remove any borosilicate shards that may be stuck in the bundle.

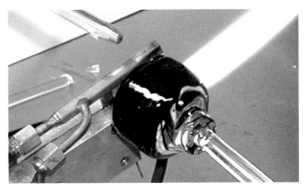

Remove the pointed punty.

13. Repeat Steps 10 through 12 on the unpuntied end.

14. Rotate the murrini bundle slowly in the flame, thoroughly heating the entire mass. Try to compress the mass. Continue to heat until the mass is pliable enough for you to rock the punties back and forth. Remove from the flame, and begin to pull.

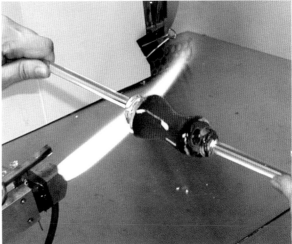

Begin to pull on the heated mass.

15. Put one end back in the flame, and heat it around the clear dome area. Rotate the glass, and continue to pull for another inch or two. Remember, you are not trying to get a murrine bundle of uniform size.

16. Rotate the other end of the bundle in the flame and pull. Be careful not to twist the already-pulled cane as you heat it. When the glass is molten, remove it from the flame and pull.

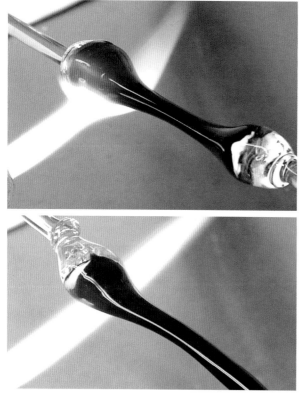

Heat and pull.

17. Cut the punty off of one end of your cane, and place that end in the kiln. Cut the murrine cane with a rod lopper into lengths that will fit in your kiln, and use tweezers to place them in the hot kiln immediately. Anneal as you would for soft glass beads.

CREATING THE MASK:

1. Create a triangular oval (see photo) for the base bead out of Dark Yellow, and flatten one side. Your bead should be at least 40 mm long so that you have enough room for facial features. You will be drawing on the curved side of the bead.

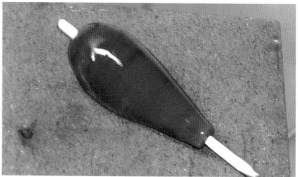

Create shape, and flatten the back of the bead.

2. Draw a vertical line running almost the length of the bead down the left side of the face, using the Dark Yellow again. Heat the area, and then marver it into the bead.

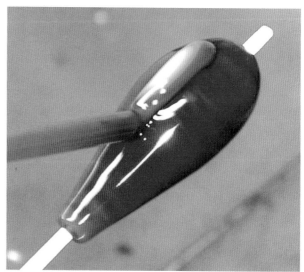

Draw a vertical line.

3. Outline the area with a Dark Turquoise stringer (1 mm); heat and marver.

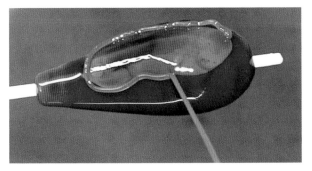

Outline the vertical line with turquoise.

4. On the right side of the face, melt in a large patch of Periwinkle. Heat and marver.

Melt in periwinkle patch.

5. Outline this patch with a stringer of Red Orange. Heat and marver.

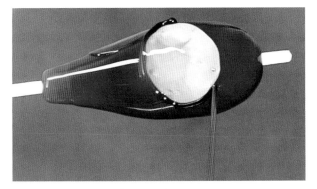

Outline the patch with a red orange stringer.

7. Draw four vertical lines of Light Turquoise across the left side of the face. Heat and marver.

Draw four vertical lines of turquoise.

APPLYING MURRINI:

8. Pre-heat the murrine for the eyes. Heat a spot on the vertical color patch until the glass is soft and glowing brightly. Pick up your pre-heated murrine, and press it down into the soft glass.

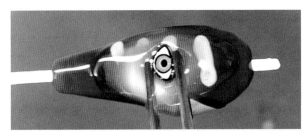

Apply eye murrine.

9. Heat the murrine you sank into the glowing glass until it is glowing around the edges. Using a marver that is parallel to the murrine, push down until the murrine is flush with the hot glass. Do not roll or rotate the bead while pushing on the murrine, or the eyes could get distorted. If your murrine is not flush with the bead after the first try, reheat and marver again. Important: In order to keep the murrine from closing in on itself, the murrine needs to be flush with the surface and melted in before continuing. Repeat for the other eye.

Marver the eye murrine.

79

10. Heat up the left side of the bead and, starting at the edge of the left side of the face where the nose is, draw a nose and bring it up and around to form an eyebrow in the same motion. Use a very thick (2 mm–3 mm) Cobalt-encased stringer. If necessary, shape up nose and/or eyebrow with a utility blade.

Draw the nose.

11. Use a slightly thinner Green-encased stringer to decorate around the eye and make the brow on the right side. Be sure to heat the surface of the bead as you apply the stringer.

Draw an eyebrow.

12. Heat a thicker (1.5 mm–2.5 mm) Cobalt-encased stringer, and touch it to the area of the bead where you would like to place the upper lip. Bring the bead closer to the flame, and draw the stringer across the bead, making a little squiggle (or "M" shape) as you go. Burn off the stringer when the lip is the appropriate length.

Add the upper lip.

13. Now it's time to reveal the Aardvark pouty lip secret! For a nice, pouty lower lip, simply heat up a thicker (1.5 mm–2.5 mm) encased stringer until you have a small, glowing glob of glass on the end of it. Drop that molten blob right beneath the upper lip and draw it across the face. Burn it off when it meets the corner of the upper lip along the side of the bead. Tweeze off any excess glass.

Draw lower lip.

14. Optional chin: If you have any extra room on your bead, you may want to put a chin there. Just add a nice-sized blob of glass far enough underneath the lips so that they don't run together.

Optional chin.

15. Finishing dots: Apply raised dots using 1 mm Black and Petroleum Green stringer wherever you think they will look best. Outline the eyes with them or run them down the sides of the bead. Dots give the bead a nice texture and can help balance out your design.

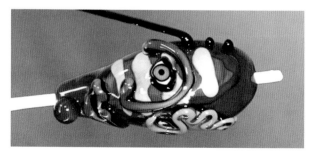

Finish adding dots. Use the "Mango Nymph" bead in the "Where's the Party?" necklace, pg. 133.

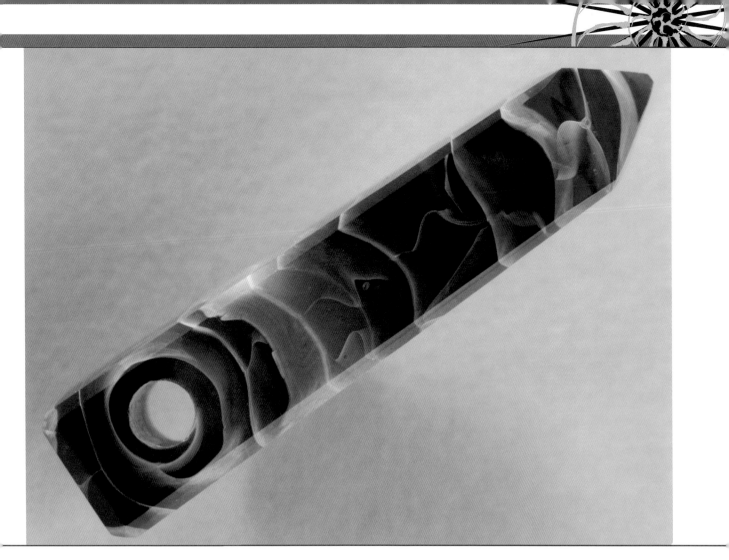

• Lampwork Artist: Kristan Child • Style of Bead: Lapidary Boro •
• Finished Size: approx. 8 mm x 36 mm • Level of Expertise: Advanced •

Mediterranean Sunset

Inspiration for this bead comes from the rich colors of the Mediterranean, such as caramel, exotic citrus and turquesa. The evening sunset leaves you dreaming of tranquility, warmth and sunshine. The "spike" beads bring out the essence of the colors of the Mediterranean. The high skill level of the bead artist can be seen in the crisp, clear cuts and angles of the lapidary work involved.

SUPPLIES:

North Star Irrid NS-14
North Star Amber Purple NS-13
North Star Caramel NS-44
North Star Double Amber NS-26
North Star Green Amber Purple NS-69
North Star Turquesa NS-15
North Star Dark Blue Amber Purple NS-49
Momka Exotic Citrus Grapefruit MB023

TOOLBOX:

Graphite paddle marver
High-quality glass dust mask
Heavy-duty grinder and polishing machine
180-mesh metal bond diamond disc
325-mesh (brown) sanding disc
600-mesh (red) sanding disc
1200-mesh (blue) sanding pad
White polishing pad and French cerium oxide
Water

INSTRUCTIONS:

MAKING THE BEAD:

1. Use a neutral flame, and start with Amber Purple; burn off the haze, and make a barrel-shaped base bead about 13 mm long.

Melt down and shape into a barrel using your graphite marver.

Make a base bead, and shape.

2. Add three parallel strips of Amber Purple on the top and bottom. Make them the width of the barrel.

Add more strips to the top and bottom.

3. Melt both sides down.

Melt in.

4. Repeat Step 2 with strips of Irrid. This is the last step to add color to the top.

Add Irrid to the top and bottom.

5. Melt in.

Melt in.

6. Add strips of Exotic Citrus Grapefruit to the bottom; melt in.

Add Exotic Citrus Grapefruit to the bottom.

7. Add strips of Caramel to the bottom; melt in.

8. Add strips of Double Amber Purple to the bottom; melt in.

9. Add strips of Green Amber Purple, and then add another layer over the top in the opposite direction. Melt in.

Add Green Amber Purple.

10. Add strips of Turquesa to the bottom; melt in.

11. Add strips of Dark Blue Amber Purple to the bottom, and then add another layer over the top going the opposite direction; melt in.

Add strips of Dark Blue Amber Purple.

12. Lastly, add a blob of Irrid to the bottom and melt in.

Add Irrid and melt in.

13. Place the bead in the kiln to anneal.

Finished bead.

GRINDING AND POLISHING:

1. Wear a glass dust mask the entire time that you are grinding and polishing. Start with the 180 mesh metal-bond diamond disc. Be sure to have fresh water running onto the disc while you are grinding your bead (never reuse water). Grind the sides to make four parallel, flat edges.

Keep an eye on how close you are getting to the hole; you do not want to grind so far down that you end up grinding right through the hole. Start on the front, then go to the back, then side one, side two, and then the top, applying direct, even pressure. Use this order throughout the whole grinding process to make sure that you don't miss a side.

Grind the sides.

2. Grind the bottom of the bead into a four-sided point.

Grind the bottom of the bead.

Hold the bead at a slight angle, and use direct, even pressure. Start with the front, then go to the back, then side one, then side two. Do not grind the edging bevels on the bottom of the bead yet, because you will have a very hard time removing the scratches that the 180 mesh grit will leave behind.

3. Repeat Steps 1 and 2 on the 325 mesh (brown) sanding disc. The surface of the bead will start to have a matte look. Go over the bead twice to make sure that most of the deep scratches are gone.

4. Repeat Steps 1 and 2 with the 600 mesh (red) sanding disc. Once you are finished going over the bead, grind down the edging bevels.

Starting on the edges of the four sides, grind the edge bevel on the long part. Do not grind the edges of the bottom point. Once you are happy with the shape, bevel the edges of the top of the bead, starting with the front, then going to the back, then side one, then side two. Now repeat the whole process over again. This is to make sure you have a nice smooth surface and get all the deep scratches out.

5. Repeat Step 4 with the 1200 mesh (blue) sanding disc.

6. Next, begin polishing the bead. Put in the white polishing disc, and add some French Cerium Oxide to the unmoving disc — just sprinkle it all over the disc, add a little water and blend it in with your fingers. Start polishing.

Grind bevel edges.

Polish with the white disc and cerium oxide.

Stop and dry the bead off every once in a while to spot-check any areas you may have missed. You will need to add more Cerium Oxide throughout the polishing process. The bevels will be the most time consuming and difficult to polish. Go over the bead a few times to make sure that you have polished all of the spots.

Use the "Mediterranean Sunset" bead in the "Geode Gems" necklace, pg. 133.

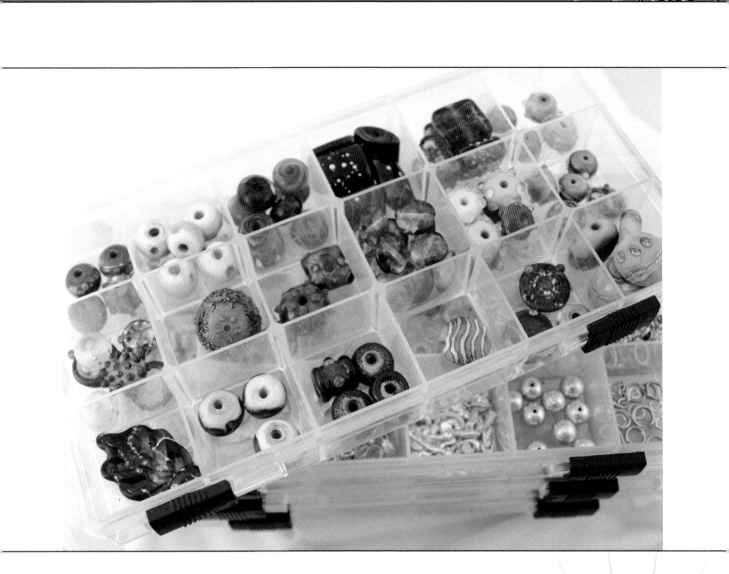

Chapter 4

Jewelry Basics: Toolbox and Set-Up

Now that you have finished making your beads, you are wondering how and what you will need to design jewelry with them. We will discuss how to set up your jewelry studio, buying your jewelry-making supplies and tools, and some basic jewelry techniques, along with some of the secrets designers use today.

TOOLBOX AND BEAD CONTAINERS

Your toolbox should include basic tools used by all designers, and it should be large enough to contain your tools and jewelry supplies, such as accents beads, findings and stringing materials. First, choose which kind of bead boxes or containers would best suit your needs. If you are using tiny seed beads, you will want to choose something that won't allow your seed beads to get mixed up in the various compartments. A screw-type lid may be your best choice. If the beads are larger, you can purchase commercial bead boxes, which are available with 5 to 20 compartments — just be sure that the lid is flush with the box. You may want to organize your beads into compartments by color, style or size. Organization is the key to happy jewelry designing. Once you have decided what compartments you want, it is time to decide which toolbox will best fit your containers and all your tools.

Tools Needed:

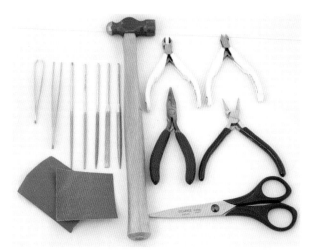

Tools.

- Round-nose/needle-nose pliers
- Flat-nose/chain-nose pliers
- Various wire cutters
- Ruler
- Scissors
- Wire-bending pliers
- Emery board
- Files
- Hemostats (clamping tools)
- Bead board
- Various glues
- Hammer

Other Supplies Needed:

Supplies for making basic jewelry.

- Bead string materials: silk, leather, cording
- Various gauges and kinds of wire
- Ear wires (earring hooks)
- Headpins
- Toggles/closures
- Jump rings
- Crimp beads
- Metal spacer beads and end caps
- Crystal and gem accent beads

All these tools and materials will get you started making your own jewelry. You may want to purchase multiple toolboxes and put tools and stringing materials in one box, bead containers in another, and wire and cords in another. If you begin with only a few supplies, put them all in one box and buy more boxes as you grow your inventory of jewelry items and tools.

SETTING UP YOUR SPACE

Your jewelry can be made almost anywhere: in front of the TV, on the patio, overlooking your favorite scenery or just lying on your bed (it is more difficult, but comfy). Your jewelry space does not have to be a professional elaborate studio; a space on a table to fit your bead board and tools will do. The end of your dining room table or a desk will work well. Some designers use their kitchen table and pack everything back up in the toolbox when they are finished designing; this portable jewelry-making works well for those with small children. Consider the chair you will be sitting in and the height of the worktable: Can you sit there for extended periods of time without being uncomfortable? Find a place with good lighting, or buy some portable lighting with the truest color possible. Fluorescent lighting may distort the true color of the beads you are using. Nothing is worse than creating a piece of jewelry and taking it outside only to realize that the colors just don't look right!

Sue Hart's jewelry studio.

BASIC JEWELRY TECHNIQUES

You will learn the basic techniques used by jewelry designers, from the simple wrap loop to removing marks on silver with emery paper. By following the simple techniques outlined in this section, you will be able to make the lovely jewelry you see in these pages. And who knows — you may be inspired to design your own creations!

Simple Wrap Loop

The Simple Wrap Loop Method allows you to make an easy loop in wire to close your end or attach to another link.

SUPPLIES:
- Wire

TOOLBOX:
- Round-nose or wire-bending pliers
- Wire cutter

1. Starting about ½" from the end of the wire, grasp the wire with your round-nose or wire-bending pliers.

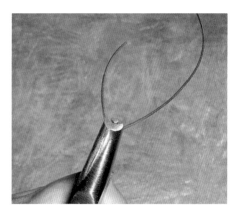

2. Wrap the long end of the wire around to form a loop on the pliers.

3. Bring the wire over and around to complete the wrap.

4. Cut excess wire.

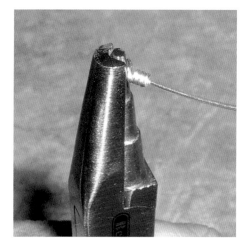

Wrapping a Briolette

Wrapping a briolette (teardrop-shaped pendant) is a bit different than just making a simple loop. You will need to string the wire through the briolette and either make a double or single loop to finish.

1. Slide the wire through the brio with enough wire left to make a small wrap, or even out the wire to make a double simple loop.

2. Pinch the wire to the shape of the briolette. Hold the end with needle-nose pliers and make a simple wrap at the base of the brio.

3. Place your pliers at the spot where you want the loop to be, and make a simple wrap as if you were following the simple wrap loop method.

4. Wrap the wire around until it meets the end of the other wire near the base of the brio to finish.

SUPPLIES:
- Briolette
- 5" 28-gauge wire

TOOLBOX:
- Needle-nose pliers or wire-bending pliers
- Wire cutter

Attaching a Toggle

The Basic Single strand allows you to string a single strand necklace or bracelet, and attaching the toggle completes the jewelry piece.

Allow a few extra inches of stringing material to finish the jewelry with a toggle.

1. String your beads. Close one end off with hemostats.

2. Add a crimp bead to the end of your strung beads.

3. Slide a toggle or clasp onto the end.

4. Bring the end of the stringing material back through the hole in the clasp and through the crimp bead.

5. Slide the string through some of the beads, cut excess, and crimp the crimp bead with flat-nosed pliers.

SUPPLIES:
- Crimp bead
- Toggle and clasp
- Length of stringing material

TOOLBOX:
- Hemostats

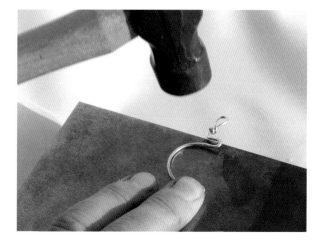

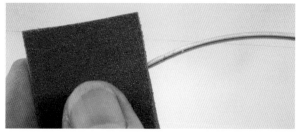

Working with Wire

There are a few secrets that will make your wire piece look more professional.

- Be careful when bending wire; once the wire is bent, it is impossible to straighten it out again without a kink.

- To minimize a kink, lay the wire on a bracelet mandrel and gently hammer with a rawhide mallet.

- If you want to strengthen wire for a clasp or for a heavier piece, just tap the wire on a flat surface with the rawhide hammer on both sides, and the wire will get harder.

- Silver wire is very soft and easily marred by your tools. To remove tool marks easily, gently rub the wire with various grades of medium or fine emery paper. Some jeweler's rouge and a polishing cloth will renew the shine.

Opening Jump Rings

Open and close jump rings so they retain their original shape:

1. Hold the jump ring on both sides of the opening slit with pliers.

2. Pull the pliers lightly in opposite directions, one toward you and the other away from you.

3. To close, bring the ends of the ring back together to meet.

PRECIOUS METAL CLAY (PMC)

Precious Metal Clay (PMC), or Art Clay, is a workable form of precious metals, either silver or gold, which contains microscopic particles of the metals and an organic binder to make it pliable enough to work with your hands. The possibilities with the material are limitless, and PMC looks great when combined with handmade glass pieces.

PMC has the consistency of modeling clay, but it needs to be worked immediately or it will dry up. Use your hands and various tools to shape and mold the PMC, and then heat it to high temperatures with a kiln or even a small hand-held torch, depending on the type of PMC used. The binder burns off and leaves the 99.9% precious metal. There is some shrinkage involved, and this needs to be taken into account when making your jewelry piece. The PMC art piece can be colored with liver of sulfur, sanded, tumbled and polished just like regular metal jewelry pieces.

Use PMC to create end caps and other decorations.

Basic Silversmith Tools

Nothing is more unique than creating your own handmade toggle and clasp. It is not as difficult as you may think. First, you will need the basic silversmithing tools.

TOOLBOX:
- Gas torch
- Heat mat
- Honeycomb block
- Flux
- Flux bowl paint brush (for flux)
- Reverse action soldering tweezers
- Files
- Solder strip

Making your own simple toggles and silver pieces makes your jewelry design unique, and coupled with your own lampwork, your piece will truly be one-of-a-kind.

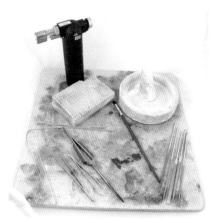

Basic silversmithing tools.

Chapter 5
Jewelry Designs

Baabs Necklace

SUPPLIES:

18"–22" of 1.5 mm leather cord for stringing
8 black opaque 8 mm faceted beads
8 twisted 6 mm sterling silver spacer beads
12 Hilltribe 5 mm sterling silver spacer beads
6 sterling silver 5 mm jump rings (2 for ends)
8 bead caps (4 mm) for yarn
4 sterling silver 2½" round-end head pins
2 handmade or purchased PMC letter B's
4 handmade or purchased PMC letter A's
4 lampwork yarn ball beads
3 "Have You Any Wool?" lampwork beads, pg. 42
1 large-hole 5 mm x 9 mm sterling silver bead

TOOLBOX:

Round-nose pliers

• Use the "Have You Any Wool?" lampwork bead on pg. 42 to make this necklace •
• Jewelry Designer: Joyce Facchiano • Lampwork Artist: Lezlie Belanger •
• Style of Jewelry: Single-strand leather necklace • Finished Size: 17½" without clasp, or as long as you want • Level of Expertise: Beginner •

This charming little necklace was inspired by adorable little sheep and fun balls of yarn, which remind me of nursery rhymes that children love so much! Just as the nursery rhymes are simple and easy to remember, so is designing this necklace. It's also easy to wear — put it right over your heeeaaaad.

INSTRUCTIONS:

1. Make the yarn ball beads ready for the necklace. Place the bead on a head pin, and add a bead cap to one side of the head pin. Place another bead cap on the other side, and wrap them with a simple loop. Add jump rings to the letters.

2. Lay out the beads and string:

- 1 sterling silver 5 mm spacer bead
- 1 black opaque 8 mm faceted bead
- 1 Hilltribe 5 mm sterling silver spacer bead
- 1 PMC letter B
- 1 Hilltribe 5 mm sterling silver spacer bead
- 1 black opaque 8 mm faceted bead
- 1 Hilltribe 5 mm sterling silver spacer bead
- 1 PMC letter A
- 1 Hilltribe 5 mm sterling silver spacer bead
- 1 black opaque 8 mm faceted bead
- 1 Hilltribe 5 mm sterling silver spacer bead
- 1 PMC letter A
- 1 Hilltribe 5 mm sterling silver spacer bead
- 1 black opaque 8 mm faceted bead
- 1 twisted 6 mm sterling silver spacer bead
- 1 yarn ball bead
- 1 twisted 6 mm sterling silver spacer bead
- 1 "Have You Any Wool?" lampwork bead
- 1 twisted 6 mm sterling silver spacer bead
- 1 yarn ball bead
- 1 twisted 6 mm sterling silver spacer bead
- 1 "Have You Any Wool?" lampwork bead (created in black for this necklace) — this is the middle bead

3. Reverse instructions to complete the other side, but be sure to spell BAA on the opposite side. The necklace should read BAA BAA as you look at it.

4. Even up the ends of the leather, and slide them through the large-hole 5 mm x 9 mm sterling silver bead to make an adjustable clasp. Tie off the ends in two separate knots.

Beach Baby Ring and Earring Set

SUPPLIES:

3 sterling silver Bali beads, 4 mm–6 mm
1 red coral briolette, 7 mm
1 gaspiete faceted briolette, 12 mm
2 orange coral rondelles, 8 mm
1 Sleeping Beauty turquoise briolette, 10 mm
1 Sleeping Beauty turquoise briolette, 13 mm
5 various Swarovski bead crystals, (2) 4 mm, (3) 8 mm
2 sterling silver beach theme charms, 13 mm–15 mm
6 Sleeping Beauty rondelles, 4 mm
8 sterling silver 2 mm round beads
1 freshwater lime pearl
1 sterling silver ring with 4 hoops
16" of 24-gauge wire
2 "Tiny Bright Beach" lampwork beads, pg. 37
2 "Beach Twist" lampwork beads, pg 22
3 Lampwork beads
16 head pins, 2" long

TOOLBOX:

Round-nose pliers
Flat-nose pliers
Wire cutters

• Use the "Beach Twist" and "Tiny Bright Beach Bead" lampwork beads on pg. 22 and 37 to create this ring and earring set •
• Jewelry Designer: Cindy Vela • Lampwork Artist: Karen Leonardo •
• Style of Jewelry: Beaded ring and matching earrings • Finished Size: Ring size 8 • Level of Expertise: Intermediate •

Nothing is more fun and relaxing than a stroll on the beaches of a tropical island. The air is warm, the sun is shining and the beach babe is having a wonderful time. The ring and earrings are very colorful with lots of movement in the dangles to catch the eye, and they are easy to make — simply attach the dangles randomly with a wrapped loop method.

INSTRUCTIONS:

RING:

1. Prepare a bead by inserting a head pin and making a half loop.

2. Slip the loop through the hoop of ring. Use your thumb to continue the simple wrap around the headpin. Trim the excess wire next to the bend.

3. Repeat with other beads chosen as desired for the rest of the loops; finish Row 1.

4. Make another row of looped beads. Wrap each row snug against the next bead.

5. Finish five rows in total. Each ring loop will have five different dangles attached in a random design.

EARRINGS:

Finished size: 2", without the hook

1. Wrap your turquoise briolette.

2. Add a lampwork bead and turquoise rondelle.

3. Add chain to the end of the rondelle and wrap with a simple loop wrap.

4. Add a silver bead and lampwork bead to the head pin, and wrap on the first large loop of the chain. Wrap the red teardrop briolette, and attach it to the second large loop. Finish the earrings by adding charms intermittently on the chain.

5. Add a dangle to the ear wire.

High-Sheen Onyx Necklace

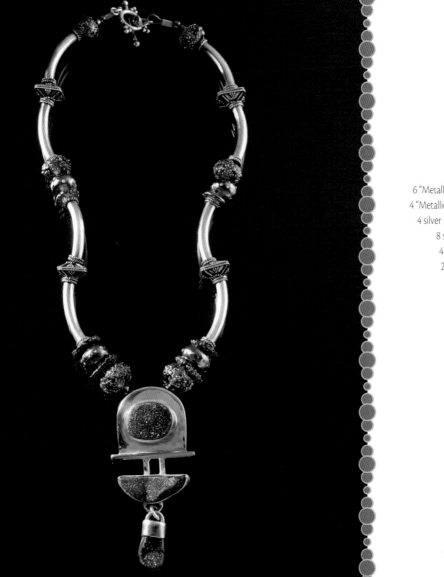

SUPPLIES:
1 Druzy pendant
11 #8 pewter-colored seed beads
6 "Metallic Silver Black" lampwork beads, pg. 23 (8 mm x 12 mm)
4 "Metallic Silver Frit Disc" lampwork discs, pg. 28 (3 mm x 14 mm)
4 silver sheen fine silver dot lampwork beads, 7 mm x 11 mm
8 sterling silver curved tube beads, 28 mm x 6 mm
4 square sterling silver Bali beads, 5 mm x 12 mm
2 silver sugared lampwork discs, 3 mm x 10 mm
4 sterling silver crimp beads, 2 mm
1 sterling silver toggle clasp
3 sterling soldered jump rings, 5 mm
20" beading wire (diameter .019", medium)

TOOLBOX:
Ruler
Bead board
Flat-nose pliers
Wire cutters
Needle-nose pliers

• Use "Metallic Silvered Black" beads on pg. 25 and "Metallic Silver Frit Disc" beads on pg. 28, to create this necklace •
• Jewelry Designer and Lampwork Artist: Karen Leonardo • Style of Jewelry: Single-strand necklace •
• Finished Size: 16" with clasp • Level of Expertise: Beginner •

This beautiful necklace uses black, silver and transparent gray as a basis. The silver sheen on the lampwork beads pulls the silver components and the sparkle in the focal together. You always need a necklace in your collection that goes with anything, and this lovely black piece is as classic as a string of pearls.

INSTRUCTIONS:

1. Lay out your beads as follows on the bead board, starting with the pendant and moving left.

- Six #8 pewter-colored seed beads. Pendant will slide over the beads.
- 8 mm x 12 mm silver sugared gray lampwork bead
- 3 mm x 14 mm silver sugared gray lampwork disc
- 7 mm x 11 mm silver sheen fine silver dot lampwork bead
- 3 mm x 14 mm silver sugared lampwork disc
- 28 mm x 6 mm sterling silver curved tube bead
- 5 mm x 12 mm square sterling silver Bali bead
- 28 mm x 6 mm sterling silver curved tube bead
- 3 mm x 10 mm silver sugared lampwork disc
- 7 mm x 11 mm silver sheen fine silver dot lampwork bead
- 8 mm x 12 mm silver sugared gray lampwork bead
- 28 mm x 6 mm sterling silver curved tube bead
- 5 mm x 12 mm square sterling silver Bali bead
- 28 mm x 6 mm sterling silver curved tube bead
- 8 mm x 12 mm silver sugared gray lampwork bead
- Two #8 pewter-colored seed beads
- Two 2 mm sterling silver crimp beads
- 5 mm sterling soldered jump ring

Follow the same sequence, starting with Step 2 and moving right.

2. Take your 20" beading wire (diameter .019 in. medium), and add the soldered jump ring and two crimp beads to one end of the beading wire. Loop your beading wire through the jump ring, and bring it back through your crimp beads. Take your flat-nose pliers and flatten the crimp beads tightly. This will make it easier to string your necklace, and you won't lose all of your beads if you drop it.

3. Begin to string your beads in sequence from left to right or end to end. Be sure to hold your project over the bead board so you don't lose beads. The pendant slides over the six #8 seed beads.

4. Finish the necklace by adding the last two crimp beads, and then sliding the wire through the loop of the soldered jump ring. Pull the beads tight against the crimp beads so you don't leave a big space where the beads slide around. Flatten the crimp beads with the flat-nose pliers. Cut excess wire with wire cutters. Now, all you have to do is add the clasp.

5. Add the clasp. Take two 6 mm jump rings (not soldered), and attach the clasps to the soldered jump rings on either end.

SECRET JEWELRY TIP:

Use soldered jump rings with your crimp beads to secure your necklace before adding the clasp. Soldered jump rings are solid circles; they cannot be opened. Sometimes the regular jump rings will come apart and your necklace will need to be restrung because you can't slip the jump ring back onto the beading wire.

Hot Spanish Days Necklace

SUPPLIES:

3 silver heavy 6 mm open jump rings
33" bright silver chain with 4 mm links
9" x 1½" 22-gauge headpins
2 turquoise carved leaf beads, 13 mm
1 silver flower charm, 10 mm
1 white silver butterfly, 15 mm
1 silver flower bead cap, 13 mm
1 fuchsia jade bead, 13 mm
2 mookaite carved leaf beads, 13 mm
1 turquoise heart bead, 13 mm
2 Swarovski 6 mm bicone crystals, 1 pink and 1 turquoise
1 pink 6 mm bead
1 turquoise 6 mm bead
9 Swarovski 4 mm crystals, 5 fuchsia and 4 turquoise
6" 21-gauge sterling silver wire
1 silver bead cap, 7 mm
1 silver freeform bead, 6 mm
3 white silver daisy spacer beads, 5 mm
2 round silver beads, 2 mm
1 "Luscious Pink Mosaic" lampwork bead, pg. 69

TOOLBOX:

Round-nose pliers
Flat-nose pliers
Side cutters

• Use the "Luscious Pink Mosaic Bead," pg. 69, to create this necklace. •
• Jewelry Designer: Sue Hart • Lampwork Artist: Cindy Palmer • Style of Jewelry: Cascade necklace •
• Finished Size: 26" necklace with 4" charm dangle • Level of Expertise: Beginner •

This necklace was inspired by the fabulous pinks, turquoise blues and browns of a Spanish summer: earth scorched dry by the sun, vivid blue skies and gorgeous deep-pink bougain-villea flowers cascading from balconies. The jewelry piece is simple, but it complements the focal bead and allows the colors to meld together, bringing out true beauty.

INSTRUCTIONS:

1. Attach the chain for the charms. Cut 7" of chain. Take a 6" piece of the 21-gauge wire, thread the wire through a link in the chain about 3" from the end, and make a wrapped loop.

Attach the chain for the charms.

2. Thread the "Luscious Pink Mosaic" lampwork bead. Slip the bead onto the wire, and add a 4 mm turquoise crystal.

Thread the "Luscious Pink Mosaic" bead.

3. Attach the neck chain. Take the remaining 26" of chain, thread the wire through the two end links, and make a wrapped loop.

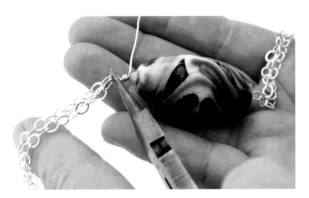

Attach the neck chain.

4. Assemble the charms as shown by threading them onto headpins or the open jump rings.

Assemble the charms.

Charm 1: 1 headpin, 1 silver butterfly, 2 fuchsia crystals

Charm 2: 1 headpin, 1 silver flower bead cap, 1 turquoise bead, 1 Bali daisy, 1 turquoise crystal

Charm 3: 1 headpin, 1 fuchsia bead, 1 Bali daisy, 1 turquoise crystal, 1 2 mm silver round bead

Charm 4: 1 headpin, 1 6 mm turquoise crystal, 1 silver freeform bead, 1 fuchsia crystal

Charm 5: 1 headpin, 1 mookaite leaf bead, 1 round 2 mm silver bead

Charm 6: 1 headpin, 1 mookaite leaf, 1 turquoise crystal

Charm 7: 1 headpin, 1 pink 6 mm crystal, 1 Bali daisy spacer, 1 fuchsia crystal

Charm 8: 1 headpin, 1 bead cap, 1 fuchsia 6 mm bead

Charm 9: 1 headpin, 1 turquoise heart bead, 1 fuchsia crystal

Charm 10: 1 open silver jump ring, 1 turquoise leaf bead

Charm 11: 1 open silver jump ring, 1 turquoise leaf bead

Charm 12: 1 silver flower charm

5. Attach the charms in the same order. Attach the head pins by making a wrapped loop. Attach jump rings by pulling them apart sideways and closing off. Space the charms approximately five links apart.

SECRET JEWELRY TIP:

You can also wear this long necklace as a choker by adding an S-clasp looped through both sides of the chain where you want it. Allow the excess to fall down your back. Try this with your other long chain necklaces too — just remove the S-clasp when you want a long necklace.

Attach the charms.

Pond and Sea Necklace

SUPPLIES:

28" silk cord
24 freshwater pearls, 7 mm
14 handmade PMC bead caps (substitute purchased bead caps, if desired)
6 water lily blossoms, lampwork or purchased
36 double-star 3 mm x 7 mm sterling silver spacer beads
2 sterling silver spacer beads, 5 mm
31 sterling silver round ball head pins
6 Pink 4 mm Swarovski bicone crystals
6 Peridot 4 mm Swarovski bicone crystals
1 sterling silver 6 mm Thai bead (or other large-hole spacer bead)
7 "Lilypad" lampwork beads, pg. 46

TOOLBOX:

Round-nose pliers
E 6000 Glue
Instant glue

• Use the "Lilypad" bead, pg. 46, to create this necklace. •
• Jewelry Designer: Joyce Facchiano • Lampworker Artist: Lezlie Belanger • Style of Jewelry: Knotted silk •
• Finished Size: Necklace: 28" adjustable • Level of Expertise: Beginner •

The water lily beads in this necklace are fluid, as if the colorful flowers are coming right out of the water. The beads are positioned in the design so that the flowers are always facing up, stretching toward the sun. The pond lilies meet with the lovely pearls of the sea, entwined in nature's sea grass.

INSTRUCTIONS:

1. Glue end caps on all "Lilypad" lampwork beads with E 6000.

Glue end caps to beads.

2. Add the pearls to head pins, and simple loop wire wrap using round-nose pliers.

3. Wire the six blossom drops: Add a Peridot Swarovski crystal, water lily blossom and Pink Swarovski crystal to a head pin, and make a simple loop.

4. Wire the focal bead: Add a 5 mm spacer bead on the head pin, and then add a "Lilypad" bead and another 5 mm spacer bead. Make a simple loop.

5. Cut the tip of one end of the silk cord in the shape of a point, and put a drop of instant glue on it. When the instant glue is dry, the cord will be easy to thread through all of the beads.

6. Place the focal bead in the center of the silk cord, and string a 5 mm spacer bead on each side of the focal bead.

7. Knot the cord on each side of the spacer beads.

8. String a 7 mm spacer bead, pearl, 7 mm spacer bead, pearl, and 7 mm spacer bead; knot.

9. String a blossom and knot. String a 7 mm spacer bead, pearl, 7 mm spacer bead, pearl, and then a 7 mm spacer bead; knot.

10. Add a "Lilypad" bead and knot.

11. Repeat this string pattern so that there are three "Lilypad" beads on each side of the focal bead.

12. String both ends of the silk cord through the 6 mm Thai bead.

13. Knot each end of the cord. You can then put the necklace on over your head and adjust it to the length you want.

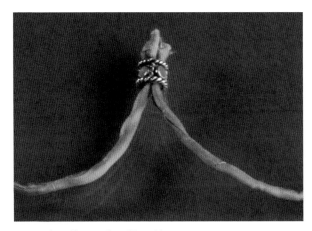

Knot each end for an adjustable necklace.

African Cat Trail Bracelet

SUPPLIES:

6 blue Czech beads

12 Czech matte gold seed beads, size 6/0

10 spacer beads, 5 mm

4 sterling silver disc beads, 7 mm

4 sterling disc beads, 5 mm

1 sterling silver toggle clasp

2 handmade oval PMC bead caps (substitute 8 mm x 14 mm purchased sterling oval bead caps)

12" stringing wire

2 sterling silver crimp beads, 2 mm

2 sterling silver crimp bead covers

Polymer clay (used in this project: Sculpey Bake and Bend clay)

10 grams .999 pure silver clay (PMC3)

Paste slip for .999 pure silver clay

Liver of Sulfur

Olive oil

1 "Autumn Glow" lampwork bead, pg. 55

TOOLBOX:

Bead mold

E 6000 glue

Files

Warming tray

Small brush for slip

Drill (bead reamer)

Sand paper

Pipe cleaner

Kiln

Tumbler

Tweezers

Exacto Knife

Round-nose pliers

Pipe cleaner

Steel wire brush

• Use the "Autumn Glow" lampwork bead, pg. 55, to create this bracelet. •
• Jewelry Designer: Joyce Facchiano • Lampwork Artist: Sue Booth • Style of Jewelry: Handmade PMC beads single-strand bracelet •
• Finished Size: 6½", without clasp • Level of Expertise: Intermediate •

This bracelet was inspired by the colors of the African bush with the beautiful browns, ambers and touches of the purple horizon. The cute little paw print on the focal inspired the handmade PMC silver beads. As you follow the bracelet from bead to bead, you can see the path of the wild cats!

INSTRUCTIONS:

MAKING PMC BEADS:

1. Using polymer clay, make impressions of each side of the focal bead. Bake according to manufacturer's instructions.

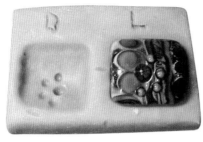
Make a bead mold.

2. Lightly coat each side of the mold with olive oil.

3. Make two balls using .999 pure silver (PMC) clay to fit the molds

4. Press one ball of the clay into each of the two bead molds, making sure that the top surface of the clay is smooth and flat.

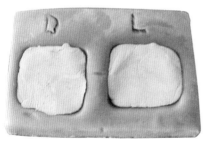
Press clay into the mold.

5. Carefully bend the molds to release the clay pieces

6. Dry the clay pieces on a warming tray until they are leather hard (almost completely dry, not pliable).

Set the pieces on a warming tray.

7. Using slip, join the two pieces together; make sure that the pattern of the bead is correctly placed on each side. Smooth the edges of the joined pieces so that no seams are showing. Return to the warming tray until the bead is completely dried out.

Join together with slip.

8. Place the bead on one of its flat sides, and carefully drill a hole through the center of the bead to prepare it for stringing.

Drill bead holes.

9. Using files and/or sandpaper, smooth out the area around the holes.

10. Fire in your kiln at 1650 degrees for 20 minutes. The clay will shrink by about 12 percent.

11. Quench the beads in water. When cooled, use a steel wire brush to burnish the bead until all the silver is visible.

12. Place the beads in a tumbler with stainless steel shot and burnishing solution, and tumble for two hours. Run a pipe cleaner through the holes in each bead, and then twist it to secure it before placing the beads in the tumbler. This step ensures that shot doesn't get lodged in the opening.

String on pipe cleaner

13. Prepare a Liver of Sulfur solution using boiling water. First, dip the bead in plain boiling water, and then dip the bead into the Liver of Sulfur. You should move the bead swiftly through the Liver of Sulfur solution, remove the bead, and immediately dip it in plain cold water. Check to see if you have the patina (finish) that you want. Repeat the process if you would like more color in your patina. Dry the bead when finished.

14. Using sandpaper, rub off the patina until the bead has the look you desire. Run pipe cleaners through the open holes in each bead again, and place it back in the tumbler for one hour.

STRINGING THE BRACELET:

1. Glue oval discs to the "Autumn Glow" lampwork bead with E 6000 glue.

2. Attach one end of the toggle to the wire using the 2 mm crimp bead.

3. Lay out your beads, and string:

- 5 mm silver bead
- 7 mm disc bead
- 5 mm disc bead
- Matte gold bead
- Blue Czech bead
- Matte gold bead
- 5 mm disc bead
- 7 mm disc bead
- Handmade PMC bead
- 5 mm silver bead
- Matte gold bead
- Blue Czech bead
- Matte gold bead
- 5 mm silver bead
- Handmade PMC bead
- 5 mm silver bead
- Matte gold bead
- Blue Czech bead
- Matte gold bead
- 5 mm silver bead
- "Autumn Glow" lampwork bead

4. Repeat the beading steps in reverse.

5. Finish with other part of toggle.

6. Add crimp bead covers to the crimps, and lightly press together.

Deep Woods Pin

SUPPLIES:

For the Main Pin:

18" of 14-gauge half hard round silver wire
1 large brown marquis bead (lampwork or purchased)
2 silver-dipped "cornflake" Greek ceramic spacer beads, 8 mm
2 brown Greek ceramic spacer beads, 8 mm
2 Bali silver daisy spacer beads, 8 mm
1 round silver bead, 3 mm
1 round silver bead, 5 mm
1 hammered wheel silver bead, 12 mm
1 "Bob's Boro" lampwork bead, pg. 31

For the charms:

2" bright silver chain with 4 mm links
1 silver leaf charm, 1"
1 heavy silver open jump ring, 5 mm
4 22-gauge headpins, 1½"
2 faceted smoky quartz rondelles, 6 mm–8 mm
2 mookaite carved leaf beads, 13 mm
1 tiger's eye cone bead, 13 mm
1 freshwater pearl, 8 mm–10 mm
3 Swarovski bicone copper crystals, 4 mm
4 Swarovski bicone Arum crystals, 4 mm
1 silver round bead, 2 mm
2 silver freeform beads, 6 mm
1 silver spacer, 5 mm

TOOLBOX:

Round-nose pliers
Side cutters
Needle file
Emery paper
Ring mandrel or suitable tube

• Use the "Bob's Boro Pressed Bead," pg. 31, to make this pin. •
• Jewelry Designer: Sue Hart • Lampwork Artist: Bob Leonardo • Style of Jewelry: Pin with dangles •
• Finished Size: 6" without dangles • Level of Expertise: Beginner •

I tried to achieve an organic form to match the "Bob Boro" beads. There are so many colors layered into these beads that it was a joy to construct this pin and choose the charms. A piece of this type is so easy to make! Change the charms for endless variations to please everyone's eye.

It's very much a freeform piece, and while you can follow my design exactly, there is a lot of artistic license in the design.

INSTRUCTIONS:

1. Shape the spring closure. Take your 18" length of 14-gauge silver wire, and start 5" from the end. Wrap the wire 1½ times around either the narrowest part of your ring mandrel or any other suitable tube (about ½" wide).

Thread your beads and accents.

Shape the spring closure.

2. Thread your beads and accents on the main part of the pin. Start onto the longest part of the wire in the following order:

- 3 mm silver bead
- "Bob's Boro" lampwork bead
- Silver Greek ceramic spacer
- Bali silver daisy spacer
- Brown ceramic Greek spacer
- Hammered silver wheel bead
- Brown Greek ceramic spacer
- Bali silver daisy spacer
- Silver Greek ceramic spacer
- Marquis bead
- 5 mm silver round bead

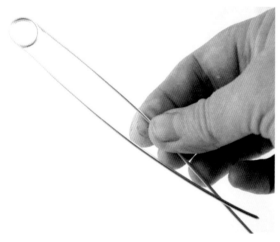

Completed spring closure.

3. Form the decorative loops and catch. Thread your short piece of chain onto the wire using a link roughly two thirds from the end of the chain — this will give you two different lengths from which to hang your charms.

> ## JEWELRY TIP:
> Silver wire is very soft and easily marked by your tools. To remove these marks, gently rub the tooling mark with various grades of emery paper from medium to extra fine. This will gradually remove the mark. Then polish with a polishing cloth and jeweler's rouge to renew the shine.

4. Using the round-nose pliers, form a large loop in the wire approx. 1" wide, making sure that the chain is enclosed in this loop. Then wrap the wire at the end of the loop around the neck of the pin where the 5 mm silver bead is located. Form a second, slightly smaller link at roughly right angles to the first. Then, pass the wire behind the main body of the pin; bend this loop up, down, and up again in roughly the shape of a curvy capital N. This forms the catch. Cut off the excess wire, and finish the catch with a small loop.

Form the decorative loops and catch.

5. Next, adjust the angles and curves of the loops/catch until the pin part of the piece fits snugly in the catch and you are happy with the overall shape and design. Take some time to make this part of the design so it is aesthetically pleasing. Once this is done, ensure that the pin itself protrudes from the catch 13 mm (½") to ensure that it can't come undone.

Adjust the shapes of the loops and catch.

6. File the point. File the end of the short piece of wire to form a sharp point. Remember: The finer the point the easier it is to wear the pin on finer fabrics. Once a suitable point is achieved, smooth with emery paper.

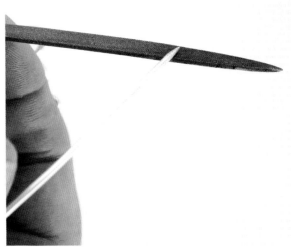

File the point.

7. Assemble and attach the charms:

Assemble the charms.

Charm 1: Thread the pearl, freeform bead and one copper crystal onto a headpin.

Charm 2: Attach the open jump ring to the silver leaf.

Charm 3: Thread an arum crystal, 5 mm silver spacer, mookaite leaf and 2 mm round silver bead onto a headpin.

Charm 4: Thread a mookaite leaf and arum crystal onto a headpin.

Charm 5: Thread a copper crystal, piece of tiger's eye, freeform silver bead and copper crystal onto a headpin.

Charm 6: Thread one arum crystal, two faceted smoky quartz rondelle beads and an arum crystal onto a headpin.

Following the design in the picture for Step 7, attach the charms. Place the pearl and leaf charms on the upper loop and the other charms on the lower loop. The leaf charm will be attached by placing the jump ring onto the loop and closing securely with your round-nose pliers. The other charms will be attached by threading the end of the headpin through the large silver loop and bending it into a small loop with your round-nose pliers. Secure this loop by wrapping the end of the headpin twice around the point where the charms sit. Cut off any excess wire, and bend down the end neatly with your pliers.

8. Make sure the charms hang nicely and form a cascade effect.

Make sure the charms hang nicely.

Night Has a Thousand Eyes Bracelet

SUPPLIES:

7 "Night has a Thousand Eyes" lampwork beads, pg. 52
5 ft. 20-gauge sterling silver wire (Dead Soft)
1 S-clasp with soldered jump rings
8 jump rings, 5 mm
24 1" head pins, 24-gauge
42 Bali daisy spacers
14 flat saucer-shaped beads
24 round sterling beads, 2 mm
8 light blue potato pearls, 4 mm
2 light blue potato pearls, 7 mm
8 smooth, round amethyst beads, 8 mm
8 Swarovski beads in Tanzanite, Amethyst, Chrysolite, 4 mm

TOOLBOX:

2 pairs small chain-nose pliers, smooth jaws
1 pair small round-nose pliers
1 jewelry-sized wire cutter

• Use the "Night Has a Thousand Eyes" bead, pg. 52, to create this bracelet. •
• Jewelry Designer and Lampwork Artist: Christine Schneider • Style of Jewelry: Dangle bracelet •
• Finished Size: 7¾" without clasp • Level of Expertise: Intermediate •

Tiny trapped air bubbles in glass are fascinating, and this set uses several beautiful bead designs enhanced with bubbles to help give movement to the lampwork beads, pearls, amethyst and Swarovski beads along with sterling silver. The colors are very soft and seductive, reminiscent of colors found outside under the moonlight.

Add transparent stone beads, create luminescence with pearls and silver metals, and add another sort of glass using the cut crystals from Swarovski. This creates a beautiful combination of colors and sparkle, which shines in the final jewelry design.

INSTRUCTIONS:

1. String a Bali daisy spacer, flat saucer bead, "Night Has a Thousand Eyes" lampwork bead, flat saucer bead and daisy spacer onto your wire. Wrap both ends with the simple loop wrap method, and cut the end of the wire.

Make the bead link.

2. Repeat Step 1, but only finish one end wrap. Slip the open end through the first link, and finish loop.

Wrap the second link.

3. Repeat Step 2 for all seven links with lampwork beads.

Continue wrapping the bead links.

4. Depending on your wrist size, you might need a little bit more length than seven beads will give you. If needed, add one extra link at each end using a 7 mm potato pearl instead of a lampwork bead.

5. Before closing the link on each end of your bracelet, add a clasp.

Wrap the clasp.

6. Make eight pearl dangles. Thread one small blue pearl, one Bali daisy spacer and one 2 mm tiny sterling bead on a 1" sterling headpin for each dangle.

Make eight pearl dangles.

7. Make eight amethyst dangles. Thread one amethyst bead, one Bali daisy spacer and one 2 mm tiny sterling bead on a 1" sterling headpin for each dangle.

Make eight amethyst dangles.

8. Make eight crystal dangles. Thread one crystal, one Bali daisy spacer and one 2 mm sterling bead on a 1" sterling headpin for each dangle.

Make eight crystal dangles.

9. Connect one pearl, one amethyst and one crystal dangle to a jump ring.

Connect dangles with jump rings.

10. Attach the jump ring with dangles to the bracelet between the lampwork links. Repeat Steps 9-10 with remaining groups of dangles.

Attach dangle links to the bracelet.

SECRET JEWELRY TIP:

When wrapping wire, be careful and accurate. Be sure to tuck in the ends of the wires around the stem so that they won't snag in your clothes. The wraps should be smooth and even for a professional look.

Take your time! If you make a mistake, then try again. Sloppy work will always show in the end, and it will make your jewelry look amateurish.

Santorini Fossils Choker

SUPPLIES:

15" 12-gauge half hard round silver wire (may need
more, depending on desired length of choker)
27" 16-gauge half hard round silver wire
24" 24-gauge half hard round silver wire
4 "Archaic Sea Disc" lampwork beads, pg. 39
1 sterling silver S-clasp

TOOLBOX:

Round-nose pliers
Side cutters
Flat stake (optional)
Hammer (optional)
Ring mandrel (optional)

• Use the "Archaic Sea Disc" bead, pg. 39, to make this jewelry choker. •
• Jewelry Designer: Sue Hart • Lampwork Artist: Karen Leonardo • Style of Jewelry: Wire work choker •
• Finished Size: 15" choker • Level of Expertise: Intermediate •

These lovely Santorini Fossils are inspired by a warm, sunny Greek island. The color of
these fabulous disc beads are exactly the same color as the ocean water that surrounds
the island.

Disc beads are very unique. They are flat, lightweight and the hole can be strung in
various ways. This set allows the entire disc to lie flat so admirers can see the entire
surface of the bead.

INSTRUCTIONS:

1. Take a 15" length of 12-gauge wire (this necklace has been made to fit a 12" neck, so measure your neck and cut the wire accordingly). The wire is already coiled, so it will form a neat circle. Form a loop 1" from the end of the wire using your round-nose pliers. Repeat at the other end. Angle the loops so that they lie flat against the back of the neck.

Make your loops.

2. Take your round-nose pliers, and grip the base of the loop where it begins; angle upwards to centralize it. Do the same to the other end.

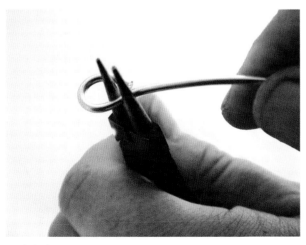

Angle the loops.

3. Secure the loops with a simple S-clasp. Measure and mark the middle of the choker to ensure that the design will be centered at the front.

Form the choker.

4. Take a 15" piece of 16-gauge wire, and place the middle of the piece over the mark; wind it clockwise around the choker base five times. One end of the wire will be hanging over the front, and the other will be hanging behind (see photo). Bend the one behind gently out of the way, because you will be working on the front piece first.

Shape the front piece of the wire as shown. It should be approximately 3" long and 1¼" wide at its widest. Then, take one of the lampwork beads, and pass the end of the wire through the hole from the back to the front. At the front, bend the wire so it goes up the front of the bead, and wind wire around the top three times to secure. Cut off excess wire, and bend down the end neatly at the back.

Position the wire and the first bead.

5. Lay the wire carefully over your flat stake or any hard surface, taking care not to damage the loop of the disc bead, and gently hammer the wire on both sides to flatten and strengthen.

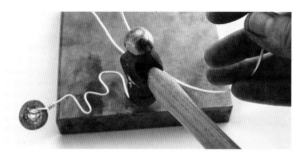

Hammer the wire flat.

6. Go back to the other end of the wound wire, and bend it down as shown. It should be approximately 2¼" long and ¾" wide at its widest. Then, take another lampwork bead and follow the instructions in Step 4 to secure the bead to the end of the wire. Repeat Step 5.

Position the second bead.

7. Next, secure the two silver lengths by drawing the shorter piece through the large loop on the longer length. The overlapping will keep the wires together.

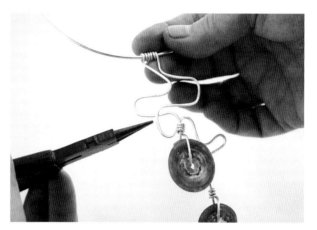

Overlap the first two beads.

8. Take a 12" length of the 16-gauge wire and wrap it around the center of the choker five times. Work on the wire that is at the back first. Shape the wire as shown, and string a lampwork bead. Run the wire through the middle and up to the top of the bead. Wind the wire three times to secure. Repeat Step 5 with this length of wire.

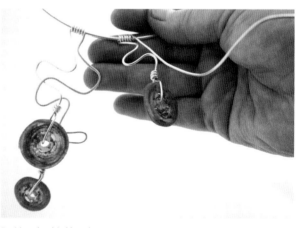

Position the third bead.

9. Overlap the length of shaped wire from Step 8 with the one on its left to secure.

Overlap the third bead.

10. Shape the last piece of wire as shown, making sure that the circle is as round as possible (use a ring mandrel or tube if necessary).

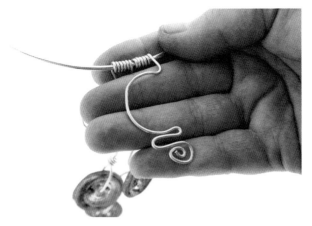

Shape the bead base.

11. Next, take a 24" length of the 24-gauge wire, and wrap the wire around the bead base six times, starting midway along the curve. Hold the last lampwork bead in position inside the 16-gauge curved wire (bead base), and pass the wire from the back of the bead through the hole, up and around the bead base; then wrap the wire around the bead base six times. Repeat until the bead is wired in, and then wrap the wire six times to finish. Make sure that the cut ends are positioned at the back of the base where they will be less visible.

12. Using your round-nose pliers, delicately crimp the 24-gauge wire into an ammonite pattern on both the front and the back of the bead.

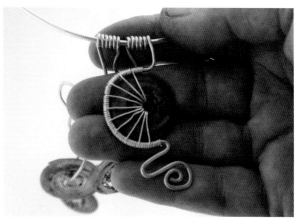

Finish the ammonite bead.

13. Try on the necklace, and adjust the lengths and angles of the wire as desired.

Make adjustments.

Casual Day Cuff

SUPPLIES:

12' 28-gauge sterling silver wire
30 "Mixed Color Stacks" lampwork beads, pg. 34
3 sterling silver square beads
1 sterling silver toggle clasp

TOOLBOX:

Flat-nose pliers
Flush-cutting wire cutters

• Use the "Mixed Color Stacks" lampwork beads, pg. 34, to create this bracelet. •
• Jewelry Designer and Lampwork Artist: Amy Cornett • Style of Jewelry: Wire Cuff Bracelet •
• Finished Size: 6" x 1½" bracelet, without clasp • Level of Expertise: Intermediate •

Create something stylish for jeans day. The cuff can be worn with just about everything —
add it to your favorite dressed-down outfit, or start the weekend early by sporting this
hand-crafted piece of art.

INSTRUCTIONS:

1. Lay out the lampwork bead pattern following the illustration on page 120, and prepare the 28-gauge wire by cutting it into four 36" pieces using flush-cutting wire cutters.

Lay out the bead pattern.

2. Begin stitching the beads together, starting with a lampwork bead from the center of the grid. Thread the four wires halfway through this center bead.

3. Choose one of the wires, and note which is the upper and which is the under wire. Add a bead directly above the center bead by threading the upper wire through the bottom of the above bead; string the upper wire through the top of the above bead. Secure the bead by tightening the wires.

Thread your starting bead.

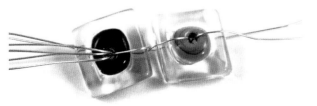

Secure the bead.

4. Add the lower, right and left beads by repeating Steps 2 and 3 using the three remaining wires.

5. Stitch the remaining beads together, working two wires left of the center bead and two wires right of the center bead.

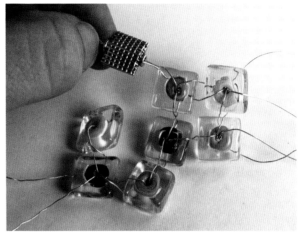

Continue stringing the beads together.

6. Thread wires through the clasp. Secure by wrapping wires.

Secure the clasp.

SECRET JEWELRY TIP:

The cuff is created using an over-under, over-under 'stitch.' This stitch is created with two methods: the two-wire over-under stitch and the one-wire pick-up stitch. The two-wire over-under stitch is used in step 3. The pick-up stitch is used to backtrack and secure a bead, using only one wire (the longer of the two wires), ending up in the same position. The stitching sequence is to secure each contiguous bead exactly once, with wires ending in the middle to secure the clasp.

LEGEND

▮ Wire 1
▮ Wire 2
▮ Wire 3
▮ Wire 4

⟩⟨ Two-wire stitch

⬭ One-wire 'pick-up' stitch

🔳 Starting point

Geode Gems Necklace

SUPPLIES:

12-gauge half hard round silver wire
18-gauge half hard round silver wire
4 heavy silver 5 mm–6 mm closed jump rings
1 heavy silver 9 mm–10 mm open jump ring
1 complete silver toggle (either handmade one or ready made), approx. 20 mm in size
5 "Mediterranean Sunset" lampwork beads (this set ranges from 15 mm–33 mm in length)
4 handmade silver stalactite beads. 2 approx. 30 mm and 2 approx. 15 mm (or ready-made equivalents)
1 handmade silver stalactite, 2¼"
20" carnelian chip beads
20" 4 mm bright silver chain
3 small silver nugget beads, approx. 7 mm–8 mm
8 small silver freeform drop beads, approx. 10 mm–12 mm long
2 diameter faceted carnelian beads, 10 mm
18 Topaz double AB Swarovski bicone crystals, 4 mm
39" bead stringing wire, 0.018 mm diameter
3 silver crimp beads, 2 mm x 2 mm
15 round beads, 2 mm
1 heavy silver open jump ring, 5 mm
1 rectangular faceted carnelian bead, approx. 15 mm x 10 mm
1 2" headpin, 20 or 22 gauge
1 silver daisy spacer or equivalent, approx. 5 mm

TOOLBOX:

Round-nose pliers
Side cutters
Tweezers
Gas torch
Heat mat
Easy silver solder
Flux
Safety pickle solution and heater
Ring mandrel or suitable tube

• Use "Mediterranean Sunset" lampwork beads, pg. 81, to create this necklace. •
• Jewelry Designer: Sue Hart • Lampwork Artist: Kristan Child • Style of Jewelry: Gemstone Handmade Silver Necklace •
• Finished Size: 16" • Level of Expertise: Advanced •

There is a marvelous cave system called Cheddar Gorge filled with stalactites, stalagmites, crystals and geode formations. When they turn on the lights, the cave is filled with wonderful organic formations that take your breath away. This necklace reflects that type of natural beauty.

Create a toggle and charm, and add the silver stalactites for contrast. Aim for something that looks as if it could have been fashioned thousands of years ago by a primitive tribe. You can use ready-made toggles and charms that give a similar effect. If you have basic silversmithing skills, then you can easily make this lovely necklace.

INSTRUCTIONS:

See pg. 91 for silversmithing tools and instructions.

1. Form two 1¼ rings with the 12-gauge wire by wrapping the wire around a ring mandrel or suitable tube.

Wrap the wire.

2. Wrap the 18-gauge wire and jump ring around the toggle ring. Wrap the 18-gauge wire and jump ring around and through the charm ring in a random design.

3. Wrap a 1½" length of 12-gauge wire with the 18-gauge wire and jump ring to form the bar of the toggle.

4. Wrap a 2" length of 12-gauge wire and jump ring with 18-gauge wire to form a stalactite.

Finish wrapping.

SECRET JEWELRY TIP:

Before you start making the necklace, lay out all of the beads you will be using. Then, temporarily thread the beads onto a piece of wire and check to make sure the design is right and that it is the correct size. This is a choker necklace, so make sure it looks good on you!

5. Place the jump rings perpendicular to the four silver pieces on your heat mat. Individually heat with your gas torch until the silver melts on the surface. This is easy to do and the metal will turn red and then you will see it turn bright silver on the surface. The 18-gauge wire will melt into the thicker wire for an organic finish.

Melt the silver.

6. Finish off. The metal will turn black as it cools. DO NOT TOUCH IT— IT WILL BURN. Pick each piece up with the tweezers and run under cold water. Then return to the heat mat.

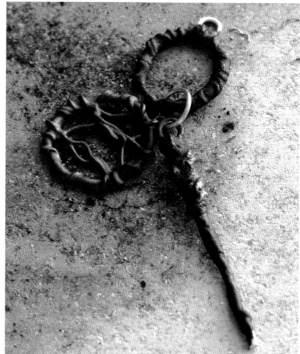

Finish off.

7. Fuse the jump ring attaching the three silver pieces. Thread the stalactite and charm onto the 10 mm jump ring and thread it through the round part of the toggle. Brush the jump ring with flux and using a small piece of easy silver solder and your torch, fuse the jump ring. Put the pieces into warm safety pickle solution. This solution will remove the oxidization and return the metal to a dull silver color. Remove from the solution, rinse and dry then polish with jeweler's rouge and a polishing cloth. The toggle is now ready to incorporate into your design.

Fuse the jump ring that attaches the three-piece toggle.

8. Cut four small lengths of wire ranging from 1" to ½". Repeat Steps 5–6, omitting the jump ring; these small stalactites will have no loop because the hole needs to be approximately 5 mm from the top. You can either drill the hole once they are formed or, when the silver is red hot, stick the end of your round-nose pliers into the metal and it will form a hole. After running the pieces under cold water, place them in warm safety pickle solution. Remove, rinse and dry, and then polish the pieces with jeweler's rouge and a polishing cloth.

9. Take your length of beading wire, and thread seven of the 2 mm beads and then one crimp bead. Thread the end through the loop on the toggle bar and back through the crimp bead, and then pull 14" of beading wire through the bead. Crimp the crimp bead with your round-nose pliers.

Attach the toggle bar.

10. Thread one of the silver nuggets through the two strands of beading wire, and thread 10" of carnelian chip beads onto each strand.

Thread the chip beads.

11. Once the chip beads are threaded, fold your chain in half and slip the middle loop over the end of one of the beading wire strands. Thread one crystal onto both strands, and then thread a crimp bead. Crimp the crimp bead with your round nose pliers to secure. Then thread the other ends of the chain onto a small jump ring, and attach it to the loop on the toggle bar. Both the chain and chip beads are now secured to one end of the toggle.

- 🔥 1 bicone crystal
- 🔥 1 carnelian bead
- 🔥 1 bicone crystal
- 🔥 2 silver freeform beads
- 🔥 1 bicone crystal
- 🔥 1 "Mediterranean Sunset" lampwork bead
- 🔥 1 bicone crystal
- 🔥 2 silver freeform beads
- 🔥 1 bicone crystal
- 🔥 1 small silver stalactite
- 🔥 1 bicone crystal
- 🔥 1 "Mediterranean Sunset" lampwork bead
- 🔥 1 bicone crystal
- 🔥 1 large silver stalactite
- 🔥 1 bicone crystal
- 🔥 1 "Mediterranean Sunset" lampwork bead
- 🔥 Repeat in reverse, finishing with a bicone crystal.

Attach the chain.

12. Return to the beading wire strands, and thread on a crystal and another nugget bead; then, cut off the remains of the shortest length of beading wire, and continue working on the longer length as follows:

13. Thread the remaining silver nugget and last bicone crystal onto the beading wire. Add a crimp bead and seven small 2 mm round beads, and then thread through the loop on the round part of the three-piece toggle. Thread the beading wire back through the crimp, crystal bicone and silver nugget. Crimp the bead with your round-nose pliers, and cut off excess wire.

Attach the rest of the toggle.

Thread the geode beads.

14. Thread the last crystal onto the headpin, and add the carnelian rectangle bead, silver daisy spacer and 2 mm round silver bead. Attach this charm to the toggle using the simple wrap method.

Attach the carnelian rectangle bead.

Growing Things Bracelet and Earrings

SUPPLIES:

Bracelet:

4' 20-gauge wire
7 "Midst of the Garden" lampwork beads, pg. 49
3 sterling tube beads, 7 mm x 20 mm
29 chrysolite faceted oval Swarovski crystals, 4 mm x 6 mm
14 flower bead caps for lampwork beads, 14 mm
10 tiny bead caps for crystals, 7 mm
2 small dragonfly charms, 13 mm x 16 mm
2 small rose charms, 12 mm
2 small leaf charms, 6 mm x 16 mm
2 cupped flower charms, 10 mm
2 large leaf charms different styles, approx. 18 mm x 28 mm
14 1" headpins
23 jump rings, 6 mm
1 fancy toggle
(Charms are Hilltribe Silver)

Earrings:

2 "Midst of the Garden" lampwork beads
6 crystals chrysolite faceted oval Swarovski crystals, 4 mm x 6 mm
2 bead caps for crystals, 7 mm
2 flower bead caps, for lampwork beads, approx. 14 mm
2 leaf charms
2 cupped flower charms
½" chain (or 5 links)
2 2" headpins with fancy end
4 1" headpins
2 ear wires

TOOLBOX:

Wire-forming pliers
Flush cutters
Flat-nose pliers
Bent-nose pliers

• Use "Midst of the Garden" lampwork beads, pg. 49, to create these earrings and bracelet. •
• Jewelry Designer: Robin Bond • Lampwork Artist: Leslie Kaplan • Style of Jewelry: Two- strand wirework bracelet and earrings •
• Finished Size: Bracelet 8½" without clasp, earrings 1¼" long without earwires • Level of Expertise: Advanced •

INSTRUCTIONS:

BRACELET:

1. Cut a 4" piece of 20-gauge wire. Make a simple wrapped loop with four wraps in it. Add one crystal, one large bead cap and one lampwork bead, another bead cap and a crystal. Leave enough room to wrap the loop four times on the end to complete the link.

Make a bead link with four wraps and a simple wrap loop.

2. Make seven of the bead links.

Make seven bead links.

3. Make three tube links by using a 4" piece of wire, stringing the sterling tube bead, and making a simple wrap loop with four wraps.

Make tube links.

4. Lay out the links according to the picture, or choose your own layout.

Lay out the links.

5. Join the links and add a toggle with the 6 mm jump rings. Place the toggle bar on one side, and place the loop on the opposite side.

Join the links and toggle with jump rings.

6. Make 10 crystal charms by adding a 7 mm bead cap and a crystal to a 1" headpin; complete with a simple wrap loop. Make five crystal charms without the bead caps.

Make crystal charms.

7. Lay out your charms, flower beads and leaves in between the links and at the toggle. Use 6 mm jump rings to link the charms to the 6 mm jump ring that joins the links. Each half of the bracelet will have a rose, leaf, dragonfly and cupped flower. The circular end of the toggle will have the two larger leaf beads. Add crystals in between each link where you like, and add four at the circular toggle.

Add charms and crystals with jump rings.

EARRINGS:

1. Add a lampwork bead, large flower bead cap and crystal to a fancy head pin, and finish with a simple wrap loop (wrap three times). Make two crystal charms with bead caps and two without bead caps, finishing with a simple wrap loop (wrap twice).

Make a lampwork link.

2. Cut five links of chain. Add the chain to the ear wires with a jump ring.

Attach five links of chain to the ear wires.

3. Attach a lampwork link to the end of the wire with a jump ring.

Attach a lampwork link to the chain.

4. Add charms, one on each link, starting on the second link from the top. Add a leaf, crystal without a cap, crystal with cap, and a cupped flower charm.

Add charms.

SECRET JEWELRY TIP:

Fill your lampwork bead with tiny seed beads if it wobbles on the wire. Slide some seed beads into the wire and inside the lampwork bead to hold it in place.

Moon Shadow Bracelet

SUPPLIES:

2 ounces sterling jump rings, 5.5 mm
5" 18-gauge sterling wire
8" 22-gauge half hard sterling wire
1 starburst toggle clasp
1 starburst bead cap
1 "Fire and Ice Flow" lampwork bead, pg. 64
8 mini Bali star dangles
3 different sterling star dangles

TOOLBOX:

Flush cutters
Round-nose pliers
Flat-nose pliers (several sizes and widths are useful)
Chain-nose pliers
File for smoothing wire wrap ends

• Use the "Fire and Ice Flow" lampwork bead, pg. 64, to make this bracelet. •
• Jewelry Designer: Cary K. Martin • Lampwork Artist: JC Herrell • Style of Jewelry: Byzantine chainmaille bracelet •
• Finished Size: 7" without clasp • Level of Expertise: Advanced •

Moon shadow was inspired by the colors of the bead, organic greys and shadowy blues. The shape and size of the bead is a reminder of a full moon: large and beautiful. The bead needs to be the main interest of the piece. The chainmaille is just the right proportions to complement the piece, and the all-silver components bring attention back to the beauty of the bead itself. Star dangles give the extra-special touch.

INSTRUCTIONS:

CREATE BYZANTINE CHAINMAILLE:

1. Start with four closed and two open jump rings.

2. Take one open jump ring, and add the four closed jump rings to it.

3. Close that jump ring. Take the second open jump ring and run it through the four you just added as well.

4. Close the second jump ring, and lay out the set of six jump rings as shown.

5. Take the two end jump rings (on the right side), and fold them backwards onto themselves.

6. Next, take an open jump ring and run it through the two jump rings you just folded back; close the jump ring.

7. Add a second jump ring in the same way, right beside the one you just added, and close it.

8. From here on out, make sets of "two in two" jump rings.

9. Use two open jump rings to attach the "two in two," and close the two jump rings. Then, fold the end jump rings back on themselves again.

10. Repeat the process attaching "two in two sets," until you have 2" of jump rings (chainmaille). Then add one final jump ring at the end you just finished, to allow easy attachment of the clasp. Make two 2" sections.

11. Gather all of the bracelet components: clasp, three star dangles, two 2" chainmaille sections, eight mini stars, two starburst bead caps, focal, and wire.

12. Construct star dangles (three different stars are used here): cut the 22-gauge wire into four 2" sections. Take one, and make a loop 1½" from the end. Add a star, and wrap closed. Make another loop, ⅛" above the wrap work you just did, and wrap it closed; nip off excess wire.

13. Repeat Step 12 using other two stars. Make a loop in the fourth piece of wire, add three dangles, and wrap closed. Make another loop ⅛" above that wrap work, but do not wrap closed.

CONSTRUCT THE BRACELET:

1. Open the single jump ring at the clasp end of your chainmaille. Put on the clasp, and with two flat-nose pliers, wiggle this jump ring back and forth 3–4 times (this hardens the jump ring).

2. Take both of your starburst bead caps, and lightly shape them around the side of your lampwork bead to give it a nice, smooth fit.

3. Take 5" of 18-gauge wire, and turn a loop 1½" from the end. Slide on the mini stars, wrap closed and nip off excess wire.

4. Slide on one of your starburst bead caps, the lampwork bead and the second bead cap. Slide the set to the wrapped loop end. Close with another loop, taking care to wrap the wire the same number of times you did on the other side; bend the loops if necessary so they are both flat and on the same plane.

5. Attach the double ring ends of the chainmaille pieces to both sides of your lampwork bead on the loops.

6. Attach the toggle through the single jump ring on the end. Add the star dangle to the same single jump ring; wrap closed and nip excess wire.

Where's the Party?

SUPPLIES:

1 "Mango Nymph" lampwork bead, pg. 73
2 complementary lampwork beads
18-gauge dead soft sterling wire
1 sterling starburst toggle
3 sterling rondelle beads, 12 mm
2 g. size 6 glass seed beads in various colors
12 various colors glass spacers, 8 mm
15 sterling jump rings, 15 mm
5 Hill Tribe swirl design dangles
3 3" sections ring-ring chain
3 Hill Tribe hammered flat rings, 22 mm
6 brushed sterling silver rounds, 4 mm
6 bead caps, 6 mm
2 stylized Bali sterling round beads, 20 mm
5 brushed sterling rondelle beads, 10 mm
1 "hat"-style sterling bead cap
3 1" sections sterling tag chain
15 18-gauge sterling jump rings, 8 mm
2 heart-shaped sterling swirl beads
2 brushed sterling rounds, 10 mm
17 sterling disc beads, 8 mm x 1 mm
2 orange glass spacers
6 sterling Bali daisy spacers, 4 mm x 4 mm

TOOLBOX:

Flush cutters
Round-nose pliers
Flat-nose pliers
Needle-nose pliers
File for smoothing wire wrap
ends (optional)

• Use the "Mango Nymph" lampwork bead, pg. 73, to make this necklace. •
• Jewelry Designer: Cary K. Martin • Lampwork Artist: Cathy Lybarger • Style of Jewelry: Advanced silverwork necklace •
• Finished Size: 27½" without clasp • Level of expertise: Advanced •

Vibrant, vivid colors just put you in a festive mood. The piece uses bold components to balance the large bright beads, and lots of heavy silver to complement and show off the color. The swirling effects of the mask bead and accents are brought out with a variety of interesting charms, beads and chain. There is definitely a party here!

INSTRUCTIONS:

1. Cut a 5" piece of 18-gauge half hard wire. Turn a loop in the wire, about 1¼" from the end. Cut three 1" pieces (about seven links) of your tag chain, and attach them to the loop. Close the loop.

Wire the tag chain.

2. Now add on your "hat" bead cap, "Mango Nymph," and an 8 mm flat sterling disc; close the other end with a wrapped loop.

Add the chain to the bead cap.

JEWELRY TIP:

To harden jump rings, take two flat-nose pliers and work them back and forth. Don't pull them open — just twist and wiggle back and forth, touching openings back each time, and keeping them perfectly together. Do this several times. You will feel the rings hardening. This process will give strength to any jewelry piece.

3. Add two #6 seed beads and a 4 mm daisy Bali sterling spacer to each of six 15 mm jump rings (18 gauge), leaving the jump rings open.

Embellish the sterling jump rings.

4. Close two of your embellished jump rings and hold them together; take two embellished open jump rings and run them through both jump rings at the same time.

Add to the sterling jump rings.

5. Attach two more of the open jump rings to the two you just added, through both at the same time, for a total of six.

Add two more to the sterling jump rings.

6. Make another six-ring set: add a sterling spacer on an 8 mm jump ring with to six 15 mm rings. Add 2 larger 8 mm colorful glass spacers to each 15 mm ring. Connect them the same way you connected the rings in Steps 4–5. Now you will have two sets of embellished jump ring clusters.

Embellish sterling jump rings.

7. Gather components for the beaded wrapped links.

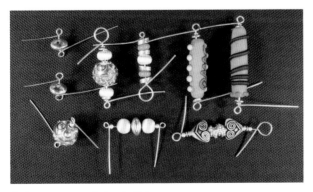

Gather components for beaded links.

8. Using 18-gauge dead soft sterling wire, cut two 3½" pieces, four 5" pieces and three 5½" pieces.

9. Make a loop about 1½" from the end of all wire pieces you just cut, but do not wrap closed. Now gather beads for your wrapped link components. (See photo for visual guide going clockwise.)

A and B. Take one of your 3½" wire pieces and put on one 12 mm sterling silver rondelle. Make two of these.

C. Take one of your 5" wire pieces and add a 6 mm bead cap, a 10 mm brushed sterling rondelle, one 20 mm stylized Bali bead, another 10 mm sterling rondelle and a 6 mm bead cap.

D. Take one of your 5" wire pieces and stack on four 8 mm x 1 mm sterling discs, an 8 mm orange glass spacer, four 8 mm x 1 mm sterling discs, a 10 mm brushed sterling rondelle bead, four more sterling discs, another orange spacer, and finally your last four sterling discs.

E. Take one of your 5½" pieces of 18-gauge wire and add a 6 mm bead cap, one of the complementary lampwork beads and another 6 mm bead cap.

F. Take one of your 5½" pieces of 20-gauge wire and add a 6 mm bead cap, your second complementary lampwork bead and another 6 mm bead cap.

G. Take one of your 5" wire pieces and add a 4 mm brushed sterling round, your 20 mm stylized Bali silver bead and then another 4 mm brushed sterling round.

H. Take one of your 5" wire pieces and add a 4 mm brushed sterling round, a 10 mm brushed sterling round, a 12 mm sterling rondelle, a 10 mm brushed sterling round and top them with a 4 mm brushed sterling round.

I. Now take your last 5½" piece of wire, add a 4 mm brushed sterling round, one of your heart-shaped sterling swirl beads, seven 8 mm jump rings and your last heart-shaped sterling swirl bead. Top it with a 4 mm brushed sterling round.

10. Finally, make a loop at the top of each of these constructed sets, about ¼" from the top of the last bead placed (to leave room for wrap-work when you construct the necklace); don't close this loop, either.

11. Gather the final components: two 15 mm jump rings, three 3" sections of ring-ring chain, five 25 mm x 14 mm swirl Hill Tribe pendant dangles, three 20 mm hammered Hill Tribe rings, the clasp, two embellished jump ring sections and the embellished "Mango Nymph" section.

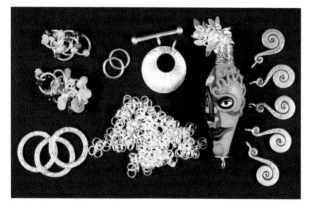

Gather the rest of the necklace components.

12. Lay the components out on your bead board in clockwise fashion, starting at the top:

- Starburst clasp
- Wrapped link component (item A)
- Bead-embellished jump ring component
- Wrapped link component (item B)
- Hill Tribe swirl dangle
- 3" section ring-ring chain
- Hill Tribe hammered flat ring
- 3" section ring-ring chain
- Wrapped link component (item E)
- Wrapped link component (item G)
- Hill Tribe swirl dangle
- Wrapped link component (item F)
- Hill Tribe hammered flat ring
- Hill Tribe swirl dangle
- Wrapped link component (item C)
- 3" section ring-ring chain
- Hill Tribe hammered flat ring
- 15 mm 18-gauge jump ring
- Embellished "Mango Nymph" section
- Wrapped link component (item I)
- Hill Tribe swirl dangle
- Last bead embellished jump ring component
- Wrapped link component (item D)
- Wrapped link component (item H)

13. Working clockwise starting with the clasp, slide on one looped end of item A; wrap loop closed. Run the open loop on the other end of item A through two of the jump rings at one end of your embellished jump ring component.

Construct the necklace.

14. Wrap the loop closed. Pick up item B, and slide one looped end through the bottom two jump rings in your embellished jump ring component. Wrap loop closed. Pick up your Hill Tribe swirl dangle and slide it on the open loop on end of item B. Take your Hill Tribe Hammered ring, slide it on your 3" section of ring-ring chain, and slide both ends of the ring-ring chain on your open loop with the Hill Tribe swirl dangle.

Necklace construction.

15. Wrap link closed. Pick up 3" of ring-ring chain, and run through previously attached Hill Tribe hammered ring; then pick up item E and slide both ends of the ring-ring chain onto the loop on one end. Wrap the loop closed. Then, go ahead and close the loop on the other end of item E.

Necklace construction.

16. Pick up item G, slide one open loop through closed loop of item E, and wrap closed. Add the Hill Tribe swirl to the open loop of the other end, and then wrap closed. Slide item F onto the loop with the Hill Tribe swirl dangle, and wrap it closed. Slide the Hill Tribe hammered ring onto the open end of item F; wrap closed.

Necklace construction.

17. Pick up item C. Slide the Hill Tribe swirl dangle on one loop end, and slide that loop onto the previously attached Hill Tribe hammered ring. Wrap the loop closed. Pick up the Hill Tribe hammered ring, and slide it onto the ring-ring chain; attach the ring-ring chain to the open loop end of item C; wrap closed.

18. Pick up two 15 mm, 18-gauge jump rings; add a Hill Tribe swirl dangle to one jump ring, and run both jump rings through the bottom loop of the "Mango Nymph" section. Then, attach both jump rings to the previously attached Hill Tribe hammered ring. Close jump rings. Pick up item I, and slide one loop end through the top loop of the Mask focal. Wrap closed.

Necklace construction.

Necklace construction.

19. Add a Hill Tribe swirl dangle to the unwrapped end of previously added item I. Run the loop through two end jump rings of your second embellished jump-ring component; wrap loop closed. Pick up item D, and attach one loop end to the bottom two jump rings of the embellished jump ring component; wrap loop closed, and then wrap the other loop end of item D closed. Pick up item H, attach to the loop end of item D, and wrap closed. Pick up the toggle piece for the clasp, and attach it to the last unwrapped item D loop. Wrap loop closed.

Necklace construction.

Glossary of Terms

ANNEAL: To hold the temperature and slow cool the glass to prevent internal stress.

BEAD RELEASE/SEPARATOR: A substance applied to your mandrel that allows you to remove your bead when it has cooled.

BOROSILICATE: Hard glass, COE 32; also called boro.

BOROSCOPES: Specialized protective eyewear used when working with borosilicate glass.

CERAMIC FIBER BLANKET: Ceramic fibers formed into a "blanket" that allows your beads to cool slowly. Beads that cool in a ceramic fiber blanket still need to be kiln annealed.

COEFFICIENT OF EXPANSION (COE): The rate of expansion of the glass when it is heated; this number is used to determine glass compatibility.

DIDYMIUM: Coating on protective glasses; used with soft glass beadmaking.

DIGITAL CONTROLLER: Controls the temperature of the kiln that you program into the controller; means that you do not have to watch the kiln for temperature changes.

EFFETRE: Soft glass, made in Italy, with a COE of 104; also called Moretti.

ENCASING: Coating the bead in clear glass.

FLAME ANNEALING: Evening out the temperature of your bead in the outer flame.

FLASHBACK ARRESTORS: Keep your flame from flashing back into the fuel system and possibly causing an explosion; important for your system.

FRIT: Small glass granules used to decorate the bead.

GATHER: The heated end of the rod; looks like a melted blob.

GLASS COMPATIBILITY: Glass needs similar COE to be used together, or the beads will shatter or crack when cooled.

GRAPHITE PADDLE OR MARVER: Smooth surface made from graphite to roll and shape your hot bead.

HOT HEAD TORCH: Basic bead maker's torch, single fuel system.

INFINITE CONTROLLER: Controller that relies on a number system, usually from 1 to 10, to control the heat of the kiln. Need to babysit kiln.

KILN: High-heat insulated oven where glass is heated, melted and cooled.

LATTICINO: Complex twists of glass made into cane and used to decorate the bead.

MANDREL: Stainless steel rods in a variety of sizes used in making your beads.

MINOR BENCH BURNER: Surface-mix torch.

MAPP GAS: Methylacetylene Propadiene, used with the hot head torch; burns hotter than propane.

MINI MASHERS: Small flattening tool.

MURRINI: Complex cane used to decorate the bead.

OXIDIZING FLAME: Flame high in oxygen.

PARALLEL PRESS OR MASHERS: Specialized flattening tool.

PSI: Pounds per square inch; psi measures pressure.

PUNTY: Rod (metal or glass) used to hold glass in flame or pull cane with.

PYROMETER: Gauge that monitors the inside temperature of the kiln.

REDUCING FLAME: Flame lacking oxygen.

REDUCTION FRIT: Small glass granules or powders used to give a shiny texture or pattern on your bead. Need reducing flame to activate.

REGULATOR: Controls the pressure of your oxygen or propane and monitors how much is in the tank.

SILVER FOIL: 99.9% fine silver in sheet or leaf.

STRINGER: Tiny strands of glass used to decorate the bead.

Resources

BEADMAKING SUPPLIES, GLASS AND EQUIPMENT:

ARROW SPRINGS
4301 Product Drive
Shingle Springs, CA 95682
(530) 677-1400
www.arrowsprings.com
Complete beadmaking supplies, glass
and equipment

ART GLASS HOUSE
3650 North U.S. Highway 1
Cocoa, Florida 32926
(800) 525-8009
www.artglasshouse.com
Complete beadmaking supplies, glass and equipment,
instruction

CATTWALK TOOLS
20 West River Styx Rd.
Hopatcong, NJ 07843-1828
(973) 398-7390
www.cattwalk.com
Lampwork bead presses and
forming trays, instruction

DOUBLE HELIX GLASSWORKS
www.doublehelixglassworks.com
New breed of 104 glass,
reactive colors, instruction

FRANTZ ART GLASS
1222 E. Sunset Hill Rd.
Shelton, WA 9858
(800) 839-6712
www.frantzartglass.com
Complete beadmaking supplies,
glass and equipment

SUNDANCE ART GLASS
6052 Foster Rd.
Paradise, CA 95969
(800) 946-8452
www.sundanceglass.com
Complete beadmaking supplies, glass
and equipment, instruction

JEWELRY TOOLS AND SUPPLIES:

BLUE MUD
17837 1st Ave. So. #513
Seattle, WA 98148
www.bluemud.com
Web-based catalog with silver
components and Swarovski crystals

FIRE MOUNTAIN GEMS
1 Fire Mountain Way
Grants Pass, OR 97526
(800) 423-2319
www.firemountaingems.com
Complete line of jewelry making tools, supplies
and equipment. Paper catalog, instruction

NINA DESIGNS
PO Box 8127
Emeryville, CA 94662
(800) 336-6462
www.ninadesigns.com
Web-based catalog specializes in all types of silver

RIO GRANDE
7500 Bluewater Rd., NW
Albuquerque, NM 87121
(800) 545-6566
www.riogrande.com
Complete line jewelry making tools, supplies
and equipment. Paper catalog, instruction

URBAN MAILLE CHAINWORKS
PO Box 682
Pine, CO 80470
(303) 838-7432
www.urbanmaille.com
Fine quality precision cut jump rings for
jewelry making, instruction

AUCTIONS:

WWW.EBAY.COM
This site has just about anything you want!

WWW.JUSTBEADS.COM
You can find beads of all types.
www.theannealermagazine.com
We offer auction service, magazine, instruction

SITES FOR INSTRUCTION AND FORUMS:

INTERNATIONAL SOCIETY OF GLASS BEADMAKERS (ISGB)
www.isgb.org
Nonprofit organization dedicated to promoting and supporting the art of making hand-crafted glass beads

LAMPWORK, ETC.
www.lampworketc.com
A friendly place to bring together glass and jewelry artists

WET CANVAS
www.wetcanvas.com
Online magazine aimed at visual artists. Features art tutorials, news, events, message forums, and more.
Search for glass art forum

THE ANNEALER MAGAZINE
www.theannealermagazine.com
Online venue dedicated to self-representing glass artists and lampwork jewelry designers

CONTRIBUTORS:

CATTWALK TOOLS
20 West River Styx Rd.
Hopatcong, NJ 07843-1828
(973) 398-7390
www.cattwalk.com

SUNDANCE ART GLASS
6052 Foster Rd.
Paradise, CA 95969
(800) 946-8452
www.sundanceglass.com

Artist Directory

LAMPWORK ARTISTS:

LEZLIE BELANGER
Canterbury Keepsakes
E-mail: beads@cankeep.com
eBay ID: cankeep
www.cankeep.com

SUSAN BOOTH
2 Cats Designs
12 Wannon Court, Melton South
Victoria, 3338
Australia
Phone: 61-3-9747-8553
E-mail: Sbooth1969@hotmail.com
eBay ID: thatgirl1269
www.2cats.cjb.net

KRISTAN CHILD
Redside Designs
E-mail: redsidej@yahoo.com
eBay ID: redsidedesigns
www.redsidedesigns.net

AMY CORNETT
AmyCornett.com
2470 Clairview St.
Alpharetta, GA 30004
(770) 442-9534
E-mail: amy@amycornett.com
eBay ID: designs-for-artful-living
www.amycornett.com

JC HERRELL
JC Herrell Glass
PO Box 1783
Oshkosh, WI 54903
(920) 216-1098
E-mail: jc@jcherrell.com
eBay ID: jcherrellglass
www.JCHerrell.com

LESLIE KAPLIN
Rush Creek Designs
125 S. Lang Ave.
Pittsburgh, PA 15208
(412) 244-9214
E-mail: rushcreek@verison.net

BOB LEONARDO
Leonardo Lampwork
362 Hood School Rd.
Indiana, PA 15701
(724) 357-8709
E-mail: justleo7@ptd.net
eBay ID: justleonardo
www.justleonardo.com

CATHY LYBARGER
Aardvark Art Glass
206 N. Brearly St.
Madison, WI 53703
(608) 251-0086
E-mail: aardart@aol.com
eBay ID: aardart
www.aardvarkartglass.net

CINDY PALMER
Full Circle Galleria
2108 E. Washington Ave.
Madison, WI 53704
(608) 467-8210
E-mail: fullcirclegalleria@charter.net
eBay ID: full_circle_galleria
www.fullcirclegalleria.com

CHRISTINE SCHNEIDER
Kiki Beads
419 Flagler Rd.
Fort Collins, CO 80525
(970) 481-3435
E-mail: Christine@kikibead.com
eBay ID: kikibead
www.kikibead.com

JEWELRY DESIGNERS:

ROBIN BOND
Lone Bird Designs
1201 West Toledo Court
Broken Arrow, OK 74012
(918) 258-0007
E-mail: lonebirddesigns@msn.com
www.lonebirddesigns.com

JOYCE FACCHIANO
Felice Argento Designs
11394 Pebble Cove
Concord, OH 44077
(440) 357-9080
feliceargento@aol.com

SUE HART
Flat 2
36 Browing Ave.
Bournemouth, Dorset
BH5 1NN
United Kingdom
07971-80412 / 01-202-303386
E-mail: sales@baublesbanglesbeads.co.uk
www.baublesbanglesbeads.net

CARY MARTIN
Cary Martin Designs
15416 Great Groves Blvd.
Clermont, FL 34714
(352) 241-6184
E-mail: PMARTIN23@CFL.rr.com
eBay ID: Lady-Seadragon
www.geocities.com/carymartin

CINDY VELA
Unique Designs by Nora
16331 Brush Meadow
Sugarland, TX 77478
(832) 818-4032
E-mail: cindyvela@hotmail.com
www.rubylane.com/shops/uniquedesigns2

ABOUT THE AUTHOR:

Karen is a proficient beadmaker who runs her own business, Leonardo Lampwork, in Indiana, PA. Karen is a member of the 3 Rivers Glass Beadmakers and the International Society of Glass Beadmakers, and she has written three study guides for a correspondence school. You can find Karen's work in "The Art and Soul of Glass Beads," "Easy Beaded Jewelry" and "Organic Beaded Jewelry." Visit Karen's Web site for beautiful beads and more.

KAREN LEONARDO
Leonardo Lampwork
362 Hood School Rd.
Indiana, PA 15701
(724) 357-8709
E-mail: beads@ptd.net
eBay ID: karenleonardobeads or justleonardo
www.leonardolampwork.com

MORE FABULOUS JEWELRY IDEAS

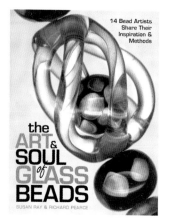

THE ART & SOUL OF GLASS BEADS
17 Bead Artists Share Their Inspiration & Methods
by Susan Ray & Richard Pearce

Step-by-step instructions and beautiful photography show crafters how to create stunning necklaces, earrings, and much more with glass beads.

Softcover • 8¼ x 10⅞ • 144 pages
250 color photos
Item# GLABD • $24.99

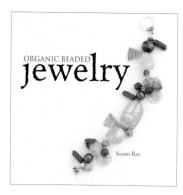

ORGANIC BEADED JEWELRY
by Susan Ray

Learn how to expand your beading expertise by exploring new materials to use. This book bridges the gap between the various materials used to create fine jewelry, and the techniques used to make unique pieces.

Softcover • 8 x 8 w/flaps • 160 pages
250+ color photos and illus.
Item# ORGJW • $22.99

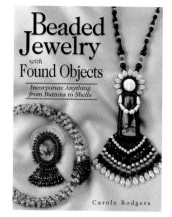

BEADED JEWELRY WITH FOUND OBJECTS
Incorporate Anything from Buttons to Shells
by Carole Rodgers

Designed for beaders of all skill levels, this striking new approach to beading involves transforming easily obtained household objects into gorgeous one-of-a-kind jewelry.

Softcover • 8¼ x 10⅞ • 128 pages
100+ color photos, plus illus.
Item# BJFO • $19.99

EASY BEADED JEWELRY
75+ Stunning Designs
by Susan Ray and Sue Wilke

For beginners or advanced beaders, this book includes 75+ projects for creating gorgeous earrings, necklaces, bracelets, pins and more. Includes a helpful resource guide.

Softcover • 8¼ x 10⅞ • 144 pages
150 color photos, 100 illus.
Item# EBJD • $21.99

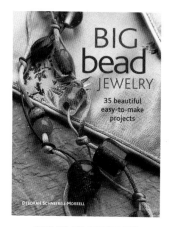

BIG BEAD JEWELRY
35 Beautiful Easy-to-Make Projects
by Deborah Schneebeli-Morrell

This guide features techniques for creating glamorous jewelry using chunky gemstones and beads in a modern organic approach.

Softcover • 8¼ x 10⅞ • 128 pages
200 color photos
Item# Z0307 • $19.99

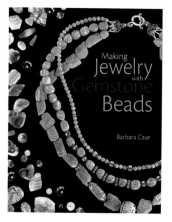

MAKING JEWELRY WITH GEMSTONE BEADS
by Barbara Case

Clear artwork, beautiful photographs and easy-to-follow step-by-step instructions ensure flawless results.

Softcover • 8½ x 11 • 128 pages
150 color photos, 250 color illus.
Item# Z1340 • $19.99